THE SCHWEICH LECTURES
AND BIBLICAL ARCHAEOLOGY

THE SCHWEICH LECTURES
AND BIBLICAL ARCHAEOLOGY

Graham Davies, FBA

Professor of Old Testament Studies,
University of Cambridge

THE SCHWEICH LECTURES
OF THE BRITISH ACADEMY

Centenary Lecture 2008

Published for THE BRITISH ACADEMY
By OXFORD UNIVERSITY PRESS

Oxford University Press, Great Clarendon Street, Oxford OX2 6DP

Oxford New York

Auckland Cape Town Dar es Salaam Hong Kong Karachi Kuala Lumpur Madrid
Melbourne Mexico City Nairobi New Delhi Shanghai Taipei Toronto

With offices in
Argentina Austria Brazil Chile Czech Republic France Greece
Guatemala Hungary Italy Japan Poland Portugal Singapore
South Korea Switzerland Thailand Turkey Ukraine Vietnam

Published in the United States
By Oxford University Press Inc., New York

British Library Cataloguing in Publication Data
Data available

Library of Congress Cataloging in Publication Data
Data available

Typeset by
Keystroke, Station Road, Codsall, Wolverhampton
Printed in Great Britain on acid-free paper by
CPI Antony Rowe, Chippenham, Wiltshire

ISBN 978–0–19–726487–4

Contents

Illustrations

Plates

12. Edward Ullendorff's lectures of 1967 have remained continuously in print since 1968; a paperback edition was published in 1988.

Figure

Preface

This book has its origin in the invitation of the British Academy for me to give a lecture on archaeology and the Bible to celebrate the centenary of the first Schweich Lectures in 1908. It seemed important to me that such a lecture should not only address some current issues in 'biblical archaeology' but provide an account of the origin of the lecture series and of its own history. It was from these combined concerns that the title given to the lecture arose: 'Archaeology and the Bible: A Broken Link?' Much of the lecture (delivered on 4 November 2008) now appears, in an amplified form but under the same title, in chapter 3 of this book. In the course of my preparation, however, I came across an unexpected quantity of evidence both about the Schweich family itself and about the Academy's own reception of what was its first major benefaction. The staff of the Academy, in particular its Publications Officer James Rivington, were kind enough to encourage me not only to include some of this material in my lecture but to enlarge its publication to form a book of a comparable size to the regular volumes of Schweich lectures. In accordance with this pattern I have divided the text into the normal three chapters, even though this makes the final chapter longer than the other two put together. It also seemed appropriate to include some documentary material as appendices to the first two chapters, and I am grateful to James Rivington for compiling a full list of the lectures given in the first hundred years, together with details (where appropriate) of their publication. This list was of enormous help to me in preparing the lecture and the third chapter of this book.

My thanks are due, first and foremost, to the Council and the Schweich Lectures Committee of the Academy for the honour of being invited to lecture on that very special occasion. Among the staff of the Academy, Peter Brown (formerly its Secretary and now its Archivist), James Rivington and Angela Pusey were especially helpful to me in finding documents in the

Academy's archives and publications which shed light on the origins and history of the Schweich Lectures. I should like also to thank a number of teachers, colleagues, and friends, archaeologists and biblical scholars alike (a few, both), for their guidance and companionship over many years: without their help I could not have undertaken the task assigned to me. Most of their names appear somewhere in the footnotes of this volume: the others will know that I include them in this tribute.

I am also most grateful to the staff of several archives and libraries for supplying me with relevant material and giving permission for its use in this book: the Cheshire Archives and Local Studies for items from the Brunner, Mond (ICI) collection; Princeton University Library for letters from Constance Schweich in the Sir Israel Gollancz collection; the City of Westminster Archives for documents and photographs in the Grove House collection; the Fitzwilliam Museum, Cambridge, for information about items received from Constance Goetze (as she then was) in 1943 and 1951; and above all, as in nearly all my published work, the University Library in Cambridge, which has such rich resources and makes them so easily accessible to its readers.

Graham Davies
Cambridge
January 2010

Acknowledgements

The British Academy wishes to thank the following for permission to reproduce illustrations.

Cheshire Archives and Local Studies for Letter from Leopold Schweich to Ludwig Mond of 9 September 1884 (Plate 2), deposited in the Cheshire Record Office and reproduced with the permission of Cheshire Shared Services and the owner/depositor to whom copyright is reserved.

City of Westminster Archives Centre for Painting of Constance Goetze (née Schweich) in Florentine dress (Plate 6) and Constance Goetze with Queen Elizabeth (Plate 7).

At the Löwenthals in 1861 (Plate 1) and The Brunners and the Monds, 1898 (Plate 4) are both from J. M. Cohen, *The Life of Ludwig Mond* (London, Methuen, 1956), facing p. 41 and facing p. 192 respectively. Every effort was made to contact the present copyright holder but without success. The British Academy will be pleased to make full acknowledgement in a future edition if notified in writing.

Princeton University Library for Letter from Constance Schweich to Israel Gollancz of 10 January 1907 (Plate 5); and for permission to reproduce in Appendix 1 translations of two letters from the Sir Israel Gollancz Correspondence, Manuscripts Division, Department of Rare Books and Special Collections, Princeton University Library.

The portrait of S. R. Driver (Plate 9) is from *A Century of British Orientalists 1902–2001*, ed. C. E. Bosworth (Oxford, Oxford University Press for the British Academy).

All other illustrations are the work of the author.

Chapter 1

The Schweich Family

A NATURAL QUESTION TO ASK on the occasion of a centenary is: why do we have something to celebrate at all? Hitherto very little has been known about the source of the benefaction which established the Schweich Lectures of the British Academy. The founding documents tell us that the lectures were named in memory of one Leopold Schweich and were to be 'for the furtherance of research in the archaeology, art, history, languages and literature of Ancient Civilization, with reference to Biblical Study'. The Academy's records from the time indicate that Leopold Schweich 'of Paris' had recently died in 1906, and Israel Gollancz, the first Secretary of the Academy, described the donor, his daughter Miss Constance Schweich, only as 'my friend' in a letter. One could also infer from the size of the gift— £10,000, which in today's money would be equivalent to fifty or more times that amount—that she was a woman of considerable means, probably as a result of her father's bequest to her. The standard reference works contain nothing of obvious value for filling out these bare details (but see below).

There is, however, a variety of source material which makes it possible to place the Schweich family in their social and historical context, or rather contexts. There remain many gaps, but the basic outline is now clear.[1]

Leopold Schweich and his Family

Leopold Schweich must have been born about 1840 and probably came from a Jewish family in Kassel, Germany, like the better known Mond family,

---

[1] An earlier version of this chapter, with only minimal bibliographical references, was published as 'Leopold Schweich and his Family', in *British Academy Review* 12 (January 2009), 53–7. Many of the items used here were first traced by searches of the Internet using Google™, but I have subsequently been able to examine most of them in a printed form.

with whom he and his children had a variety of connections.[2] In February 1862 he married Philippina Mond (1840–73), a cultured young woman and the sister of Ludwig Mond, who was himself to become a great chemist and industrialist in England, being the founder or joint founder of the companies which eventually became ICI.[3] J. M. Cohen, the biographer of Ludwig Mond, had access to a vast archive of the latter's correspondence, which included, it seems, a good deal of information about the Schweichs. From Cohen's incidental references to Leopold it is possible to fill out what is known of him from other sources, though detailed information about his parents, birth and home is still lacking.[4] There may be more in the archive that Ludwig Mond's biographer saw no reason to include. A photograph from 1861 (opposite p. 41) shows Leopold with Ludwig Mond, the latter's future wife (Frida Löwenthal) and her parents (Plate 1).

Leopold was in Cologne before his marriage and planned to make it the family home (pp. 56–7). His own wedding took place in the Mond home at Kassel with a rabbi present and the honeymoon was in Paris (pp. 58–9). Leopold Schweich was a successful businessman in the international jewellery trade, and achieved some wealth, but he was regarded by the Monds as unreliable (p. 95). He had a reputation as a *bon viveur* (p. 114) and seems to have required good entertainment from the more withdrawn Ludwig on a visit to Utrecht in 1863 (p. 99). The family were still in Cologne in 1865 and Leopold (and presumably his wife and first child) attended Ludwig Mond's wedding in October 1866 (p. 114).

Leopold and Philippina had two children before her early death in 1873, Emil(e) (b. 1865) and Constance (b. 1869). Possibly by the time of Constance's birth the Schweichs were already in Paris.[5] In the 1870s Ludwig,

---

2 J. Goodman, *The Mond Legacy: A Family Saga* (London, Weidenfeld and Nicolson, 1982), p. 18, describes him as 'of Cologne' at the time of his marriage, but this need not exclude an upbringing in Kassel, which his early close friendship with Ludwig Mond makes likely.

3 For the date see Goodman, *Mond Legacy*, p. 19; Philippina's cultural interests are illustrated in a letter cited by J. L. Rischbieter, *Henriette Hertz: Mäzenin und Gründerin der Bibliotheca Hertziana in Rom* (Stuttgart, Franz Steiner, 2004), p. 33. On Ludwig Mond see above all J. M. Cohen, *The Life of Ludwig Mond* (London, Methuen, 1956), and also Goodman, *Mond Legacy, passim*; *Dictionary of National Biography*, 2nd Supp., ii, 631–4; and Rischbieter, *Henriette Hertz*, pp. 31–57.

4 Page references in parentheses in the text of the following paragraphs are to Cohen, *Life*.

5 Emile Schweich's obituary in *Journal of the Chemical Society* 1939/1, 729–31 (with photograph), states that he 'spent his early years' there.

who had by this time settled in the north of England, lost faith in Leopold and increasingly took his children under his wing (p. 151): Leopold's absences on business trips abroad (even to Russia), as well as the death of Philippina, seem to have played a part in this (p. 163; cf. p. 95). But they remained in contact and two letters from Leopold to Ludwig (and in the first case also his wife Frida), dated April and September 1884, survive in the ICI (Brunner, Mond) archives in Chester.[6] These provide us with his address in Paris at the time, 8 rue Martel, near the Gare du Nord and Gare de l'Est, and from the printed letterhead of one we also learn that this was the base for 'Schweich Frères', presumably his family business (Plates 2 and 3). The same archive contains two letters (dated August and September 1884) from a Louis Schweich to Ludwig Mond, one of which carries the address '119 (altered from '107') Boulevard de Magenta', which was nearby: he is presumably Leopold's brother, or one of them. A topic in all four of these letters is the Schweich brothers' wish to invest in the Mond company, which was greatly expanding its operations at this time. Both Leopold's letters contain references to Constance ('meine geliebte Constance' in one), but they also suggest that even at the age of fifteen she was not living regularly with him. Emile (see below) was already away studying in Zürich. The last we know of Leopold before his death is that he invested in the company which his son Emile set up in Jamaica, probably in the 1890s.[7]

Emile was educated at the Collège de Sainte Barbe and the Lycée Condorcet in Paris and then at the Polytechnicum in Zürich. His obituary contains a story from his student days which reflects his father's strictness with him (but also his sense of humour):

> Like many parents at that period, Emile Mond's father did not believe in pampering his children. One story of his Zürich days Emile Mond has related with his characteristic appreciation of delicate humour. Always abstemious, he nevertheless found it trying at times to be deprived of an occasional glass of wine to accompany his boarding-house fare. Then came an opportunity and after some hesitation he wrote to his father suggesting a small supplement to his allowance in order to purchase a little wine which would render the dubious liquid from the municipal water-tap more safe during the prevailing epidemic of typhoid in Zürich. Replying immediately, his father pointed out that a few drops of vinegar would be at least as effective if not more so for the purpose![8]

6 Brunner, Mond and Co. Ltd Archives, in the Cheshire Archives, DIC/BM/7/5, cited with permission.
7 Cohen, *Life*, p. 192.
8 *Journal of the Chemical Society* 1939, 1, 729.

In the Brunner, Mond archive mentioned above there is also a letter, dated June 1884, from Emile Schweich to Ludwig Mond, written from Zürich. It is a long letter, in which Emile describes the scientific courses that he was following at the Polytechnicum, but also reports on a study visit which he and other students had made to Italy and seeks his uncle's advice about some aspects of his studies. Clearly the relationship was already a close and valued one. Emile went on to become a successful chemist like the Monds and was given a job in the family firm.[9] At some point he took the name Mond (apparently by 1916: see below on his wife), being known as Emile Schweich Mond. He was Vice-President of the Chemical Society (1929–31) and its Treasurer from 1931 until his death in 1938.

Constance had also joined the Monds in England by 1894, where it is said that she lived with them as 'almost a daughter'.[10] In 1892 she was with the renowned Jewish patron of culture Henriette Her(t)z on visits to Bayreuth and Frankfurt. Hertz, who was now 46, apparently acted as a chaperone to the younger Constance.[11] Their association no doubt came about through the Monds, as Hertz and Frida Mond had been at school together in Cologne. Hertz and the Monds were in regular close contact again from 1868 onwards. In her later years this continued and she was often with them in London and in Rome until her death in 1913.[12]

Both Emile and Constance were present at the twenty-fifth anniversary of the foundation of Brunner, Mond in 1898 (Plate 4).[13] Both of them were to marry children of James Henry Goetze, a London coffee merchant. This was also the family of the Violet who had become the wife of Alfred Mond, Ludwig's younger son, in 1892 (1894 according to the *Dictionary of National Biography*).[14] In 1894 Emile married Angela Goetze, and they had five children: she is likely to be the Angela Mond who founded the British Academy's Italian Lectures in 1916 (Emile must therefore have taken the

9 Cohen, *Life*, pp. 190–1, 241, 246–7.
10 Cohen, *Life*, pp. 183, 190–1.
11 Rischbieter, *Henriette Hertz*, pp. 177–8. Rischbieter's book provides a full account of Hertz's life and benefactions, based on extensive archives. Again it is possible that these may contain more information, especially about Constance.
12 Rischbieter, *Henriette Hertz*, p. 31 and n. 75 (school); p. 175 (contact from 1868); p. 57 (later years).
13 Cohen, *Life*, opposite p. 192.
14 On him see *Dictionary of National Biography* 1922–30, pp. 602–5, also Goodman, *Mond Legacy*, passim.

surname Mond by then). Frida Mond, Ludwig's wife, was another benefactor of the Academy, endowing the Warton and Shakespeare Lectures in 1910 (in memory of Ludwig, who had died in the previous year?) and what is now the Gollancz Lecture, which was first given in 1924, the sixtieth year of Israel (by then Sir Israel) Gollancz, whom she greatly admired. Frida Mond died in 1923, and the endowment was a bequest in her will.[15] Her friend Henriette Hertz had also made a benefaction to the Academy in her will: the Henriette Hertz Fund supports the 'Master Mind', Philosophical and Aspect of Art Lectures.[16]

Constance Schweich, her Marriage and her Other Benefactions

Some correspondence between Constance Schweich and Israel Gollancz survives (see the Appendix to this chapter and Plate 5) and it shows that early in 1907 she was in Frankfurt and attending lectures at the Akademie für Sozial- und Handelswissenschaft (which later became the University of Frankfurt) on French and English literature, German history, Italian and Experimental Psychology. Her use of headed notepaper with the address and in one case her initials printed implies that the stay was a lengthy one. An intriguing possibility is that the house (67 Beethovenstrasse) had belonged to her late father. Although in nearly all references to him in print he is described as 'Leopold Schweich of Paris', the notice of the marriage of Emile Schweich in 1894 stated that he was the only son of Leopold Schweich 'of Paris and Frankfort [sic]'.[17] This must point to his having a residence there, probably combined with a branch of the family business.

---

15 Goodman, *Mond Legacy*, p. 120.
16 On the wider context, philanthropic, social and economic, of these gifts in German-Jewish life in early twentieth-century England see W. E. Mosse *et al.* (eds), *Second Chance: Two Centuries of German-Speaking Jews in the United Kingdom* (Tübingen, J. C. B. Mohr, 1991), especially T. M. Endelman, 'German-Jewish Settlement in Victorian England' (pp. 37–56), and P. Alter, 'German-Speaking Jews as Patrons of the Arts and Sciences in Edwardian England' (pp. 209–19); and Rischbieter, *Henriette Hertz, passim*.
17 *The Times*, 9.10.1894, p. 1. The brief account of Henriette Hertz's visit to Frankfurt 'mit Constance Schweich' (Rischbieter, *Henriette Hertz*, p. 178) might also indicate that the Schweichs had a house there where Constance sometimes lived.

To judge from the letter of 10 January 1907 Constance had plenty of space for guests, which suggests more than a small apartment.

The letters also show that at this time Constance and Gollancz were indeed on good terms, extending to the giving of a gift, the hope of visits (at least on her part) and some informality and mutual amusement, not to say affection. One might even wonder if there was thought to be a prospect of a more lasting attachment. But if so, it came to nothing. Instead, in September 1907, Constance's engagement to Sigismund Goetze was announced. He was a painter of some repute who had long been known to the Monds (since 1891) and to Constance: she was already his sister-in-law.[18] He was later commissioned to paint murals at the Foreign Office during the First World War.[19] In addition to the normal reference to her (late) father the announcement called her 'the niece of Dr. Ludwig Mond F.R.S.', which reflected her place in the Mond family circle. The wedding was at St Stephen's Church on Avenue Road, St John's Wood, which was next door to the Monds' London house, 'The Poplars'. It took place on 23 October, less than a month after the announcement of the engagement.[20] At the time of their marriage Constance was 38. It is possible that she had taken over Henriette Hertz's lifelong abhorrence of marriage,[21] but if so her father's death seems to have changed matters.

As their home Sigismund Goetze bought the lease of Grove House, a mansion at the north-west corner of Regent's Park, opposite St John's (Wood) Church and a short distance from the Mond residence at 20 Avenue Road. Papers about the house are preserved in the City of Westminster archives, and include a photograph of a painting of Constance in Florentine dress by her husband (1911; Plate 6), a wartime photograph of her, and photographs of a garden party at the house in July 1939 at which the Queen (i.e. the Queen

18 Goodman, *Mond Legacy*, pp. 57–8—he is also in the 1898 photograph (Fig. 4), not far from Constance.

19 Sigismund Goetze, *Mural Decorations at the Foreign Office: Descriptive Account by the Artist* (London, repr. 1936). He also gave, at first anonymously, £1000 towards the cost of the facsimile edition of the Old Testament section of Codex Sinaiticus, published in 1922 on behalf of the British Academy (F. G. Kenyon, *The British Academy: The First Fifty Years* [London, British Academy and Oxford University Press, 1952], pp. 19–20).

20 *The Times*, 28.9.1907, p. 10; 25.10.1907, p. 1. Gollancz was engaged shortly afterwards to Alide Goldschmidt, the niece of Henriette Hertz (Cohen, *Life*, p. 242), and they were married in 1910 (Rischbieter, *Henriette Hertz*, p. 155).

21 Rischbieter, *Henriette Hertz*, pp. 25–8.

Mother of more recent times) was present (Plate 7).[22] The house, to judge from later sales and bequests (see below), was evidently full of valuable antiques and paintings.[23] Constance had a reputation as a 'gifted pianist': she gave concerts at Grove House and accompanied Segovia on several occasions.[24] But the couple's company was not universally appreciated, it seems: the writer Arthur Symons (1865–1945) wrote to his wife in 1912 that it had been good to get away from 'the Gu-ts', which seems to have been a nickname for them.[25]

In the 1940s, after her husband's death in 1939, Constance disposed of a number of items: a fifteenth-century manuscript of Pseudo-Augustine, now in the Henry Davis Collection at the British Library; and a (?) sixteenth-century miniature of the Crucifixion, a wooden statue of St Christopher c. 1500, another of a female saint, four female saints c. 1480–1500, a seventeenth-century St John, a nineteenth-century St Helen, a fifteenth-century angel, an eighteenth-century Assumption of the Virgin and a sixteenth-century *Christus lapsus*, all now in the Fitzwilliam Museum.[26]

In 1944 Constance set up a fund, named after her, to improve public parks by the erection of works of ornamental sculpture. It is referred to in Hansard for 23 July 1957, in connection with a decision to install an ornamental fountain in Hyde Park ('Joy of Life' by T. B. Huxley-Jones), which was to be paid for by the Constance Fund. Much more information about the Fund and the family is given in a booklet about the sculpture of

22 City of Westminster Archives Centre, Grove House/Nuffield Lodge Papers, accession no. 2039.
23 See also P. Hunting, *A Short History of Nuffield Lodge, Regent's Park* (Kings Lynn, 1974), pp. 25–30.
24 Cf. Hunting, *Short History*, pp. 25–6; M. Holman, *Embodying the Abstract: The Sculpture of Richard Rome* (London, Broken Glass, 2007), p. 12.
25 J. H. Stape and O. Knowles (ed.), *A Portrait in Letters: Correspondence to and about Conrad* (Amsterdam, Rodopi, 1996), pp. 81–2.
26 For the Crucifixion miniature see F. Wormald and P. M. Giles, *A Descriptive Catalogue of the Additional Illuminated Manuscripts in the Fitzwilliam Museum* (Cambridge, CUP, 1982), i, p.395, also 'Annual Report of the Fitzwilliam Museum Syndicate, 1943', in *Cambridge University Reporter*, 1943–4, p. 635; for details of other gifts pp. 633–5, 638. It is ironic, given Constance Schweich's likely Jewish origins, that these items are recorded in a list of 'suspect' objects acquired between 1933 and 1945. Sigismund Goetze was, like others in his family (the evidence is especially clear for his sister Violet: see Goodman, *Mond Legacy, passim*), a devout (Anglican) Christian, so the selection of these ecclesiastical items may well have been his. His widow, as my wife has suggested to me, may well have thought them superfluous after his death.

Richard Rome that was inspired by his 'Millennium Fountain' in Cannizaro Park, Wimbledon, which was also paid for by the Fund.[27] The original idea for the Fund had come from Sigismund Goetze, and Constance later recalled the circumstances where it was first conceived:

> We were touring in Italy and stopped at Bologna to see [Giambologna's] famous Neptune Fountain which is erected in the midst of the picturesque flower market. The day was a perfect one, and the bronze seemed alive under the sprinkling water, bathed in sunshine, against a dazzling background of exquisite flowers. We were spellbound by the loveliness of the scene, to which a busy crowd added a peculiar charm. And it set my husband wondering why our sculptors in England are so rarely given the opportunity of displaying their works in open spaces, in parks and recreation grounds, where the man in the street can enjoy them and, may be, gain love and understanding for works of lasting value and real artistic merit.[28]

In addition to those already mentioned, the Fund paid for fountains in Regent's Park ('Triton'; Plate 8), Victoria Park in Bethnal Green ('Little Tom') and Green Park ('Diana of the Treetops'), as well as elsewhere in the United Kingdom.

Constance had moved out of Grove House following bomb damage in 1941, and at the end of the war the lease was reassigned and she lived at 40 Avenue Road, where she died on 12 February 1951.[29] A Memorial Service for her was held in St Mark's Church, Hamilton Terrace, on 20 February with well over a hundred present, including the Lord Mayor and the Lady Mayoress.[30] In her will Constance left money to the Royal Academy of Music to assist promising performers on the piano or a stringed instrument to acquire an instrument for use in their first recital in a London concert hall, as well as to other good causes. The will also provided for a small chapel and a stained-glass window at St Mark's, Hamilton Terrace, in memory of her husband. In all she left £418, 452.[31] She bequeathed a number of further items to the Fitzwilliam Museum, including a bronze bust of her husband by Sir William Goscombe John, a bronze cast of Perseus by Alfred Gilbert, an eighteenth-century *Pieta*, three Books of Hours (Mss.

---

27 Holman, *Embodying the Abstract* (above, n. 24), where for more information the reader is referred to the catalogue of a memorial exhibition for Sigismund Goetze at the Galleries of the Royal Society for British Sculptors (1948). Constance's obituary (see n. 28) gives the date of the establishment of the Fund as 1940.
28 Quoted in Holman, *Embodying the Abstract*, p. 12.
29 Hunting, *Short History*, p. 20; *The Times* 13.2.1951, p. 1 (short obituary on p. 6)
30 *The Times* 21.2.1951, p. 6.
31 *The Times* 11.4.1951, p. 6.

9–11.1951) and three eighteenth-century painted jugs. These were delivered to the museum by a Mrs May Cippico, who is described (in connection with the *Pieta*) as Constance Goetze's niece. She was the daughter of Constance's brother Emile.[32] It seems that the Goetzes had no children of their own.

The Gift to the British Academy

With her close connections to the Monds it is not at all surprising that Constance Schweich made a benefaction to the Academy, only perhaps that she was the first to do so. It remains unclear, however, why exactly she wanted to support research into antiquity for the sake of biblical study.[33] Her Jewish origins may have played a part, but her relatives generally gave their support to the study of modern European culture. An interesting and perhaps significant exception is Robert (later Sir Robert) Mond, Ludwig's elder son.[34] Although primarily an industrial chemist like his father, he had a profound interest in Near Eastern archaeology, especially after being forced for health reasons to spend several winters in Egypt from 1902. He both participated in excavations and supported them financially and later he was the major financial supporter of the British School of Archaeology in Jerusalem (BSAJ) in the 1920s, including Dorothy Garrod's work at the Mount Carmel Caves.[35] The offer of Constance's benefaction came with

32 Countess (sic) May Cippico is also first on the list of those attending the Memorial Service, probably as the closest surviving relative. She had married into a noble Italian family in 1929 and died in 1980 at the age of 76 (*The Times* 29.5.1929, p. 19; 5.8.1980, p. 22). A short obituary indicates that her four brothers had predeceased her (*The Times*, 8.8.1980, p. 12), and this was apparently even before 1951. I am grateful to Dr Stella Panayotova and Dr Julia Poole of the Fitzwilliam Museum for their generous help with regard to the items held there. The three Books of Hours are described in Wormald and Giles, *Descriptive Catalogue,* ii, pp. 459–70; see also 'Annual Report of the Fitzwilliam Museum Syndicate, 1951', in *Cambridge University Reporter*, 1951–2, p. 1305; with information about further gifts on pp. 1304–6.

33 There is no specific evidence that the Academy had proposed this subject, but it is possible: there were a number of biblical scholars and archaeologists (including W. M. Ramsay) among its early Fellows. Gollancz was involved in Jewish education and might have suggested the topic.

34 See *Dictionary of National Biography* 1931–40, pp. 622–3; *Who Was Who* 1929–40, p. 954; Cohen, *Life*, pp. 117–18 etc., Goodman, *Mond Legacy*, pp. 75–6, 176–7 and *passim.*

35 See my essay on 'British Archaeologists' in J. F. Drinkard *et al.* (eds), *Benchmarks in*

detailed provisions for its use, including the support of excavations and the distribution of any objects found, and this would be much more intelligible if she were being guided by someone with the interests of Robert Mond.[36] Although the key letter offering the gift is at present missing from the Council of the Academy's minute-book, the private correspondence between Constance Schweich and Israel Gollancz from early in 1907 preserved in the Gollancz archive at Princeton University (see the Appendix to this chapter) shows that both of them were close to Robert Mond at this time. In a letter dated 10 January 1907 Constance wrote to Gollancz:

> I was so glad that you went to Paris with my darling auntie [Mrs Frida Mond] and poor Robert. My thoughts were permanently with them during the sad days, which ought to be days of joy for all! I am sure your sympathy and friendship was a great help and that the little ones were more than happy with you. Irene is a great favourite of mine.

Robert Mond's wife had died, tragically, late in 1905, leaving him with two young daughters. The likelihood of his interest in the Schweich project is increased by his involvement in the publication in 1906 of the first substantial volume of *Aramaic Papyri Discovered at Assuan* (the texts better known as the Elephantine papyri). According to his own introductory Note, Robert Mond was telephoned about the discovery of papyri during his own excavations at Thebes in the spring of 1904 and he immediately travelled to Aswan and 'acquired them with the intention of presenting them to the British Museum'. When the Egyptian authorities virtually insisted that he present them to the Cairo Museum, he made it a condition that he should have the right of publication. The Oxford scholar A. H. Sayce had seen them at Thebes and agreed to edit them, subsequently with the help of A. E. Cowley. Mond actually financed the elaborate publication of the texts and seems to have been behind the inclusion of two scholarly appendices. Although the documents included were only contracts, and not the even

---

Time and Culture: Essays in Honor of Joseph A. Callaway (Atlanta, Scholars Press, 1988), pp. 37–62 (41), and J. N. L. Myres, *Palestine Exploration Quarterly* 1939, 44–6 (memoir). As one of the four founders of the BSAJ and its first Hon. Treasurer he gave nearly £3000 towards its expenses in the opening year, and his generosity was recognised in a special motion at the first AGM (*BSAJ First Annual Report, 1920*, pp. 5–6, 8–9). Further substantial donations followed. He was also on the Executive Committee of the Palestine Exploration Fund from 1920 and its Joint Treasurer from 1930 (*Palestine Exploration Quarterly* 1939, 1 [with portrait opposite]).

36 Henriette Hertz was also interested in archaeology (Rischbieter, *Henriette Hertz*, p. 51 n. 152), and she and Robert Mond travelled together to Egypt in 1909 (ibid., p. 181).

Plate 1 At the Löwenthals in 1861.

Back Leopold Schweich, Frida Löwenthal (Mond), Ludwig Mond.
Front Johanna Löwenthal, Adolf Löwenthal.

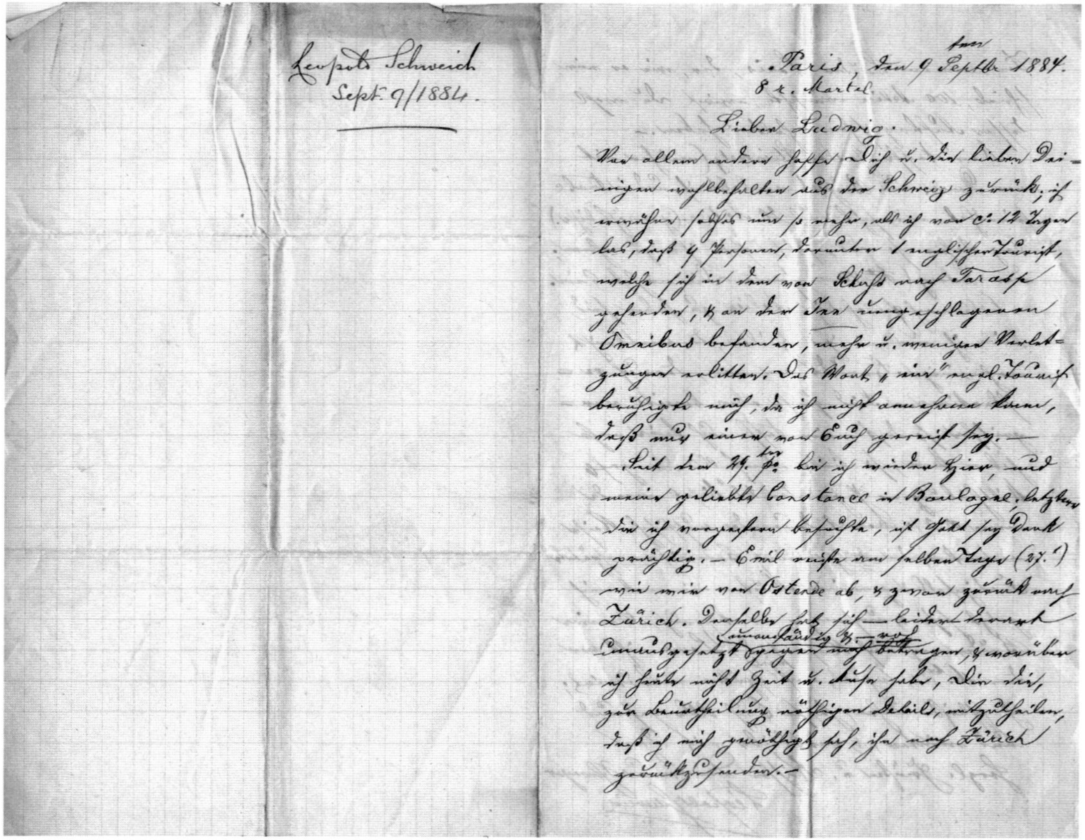

Plate 2 Letter from Leopold
Schweich to Ludwig Mond of 9
September 1884.

Plate 3 8 rue Martel, Paris.

Plate 4 The Brunners and the Monds, 1898.

Ludwig and Frida Mond are left of centre in the front row. Behind, third and fourth from the left, are Emile and Constance Schweich. Sigmund Goetze is further to the rear, at centre.

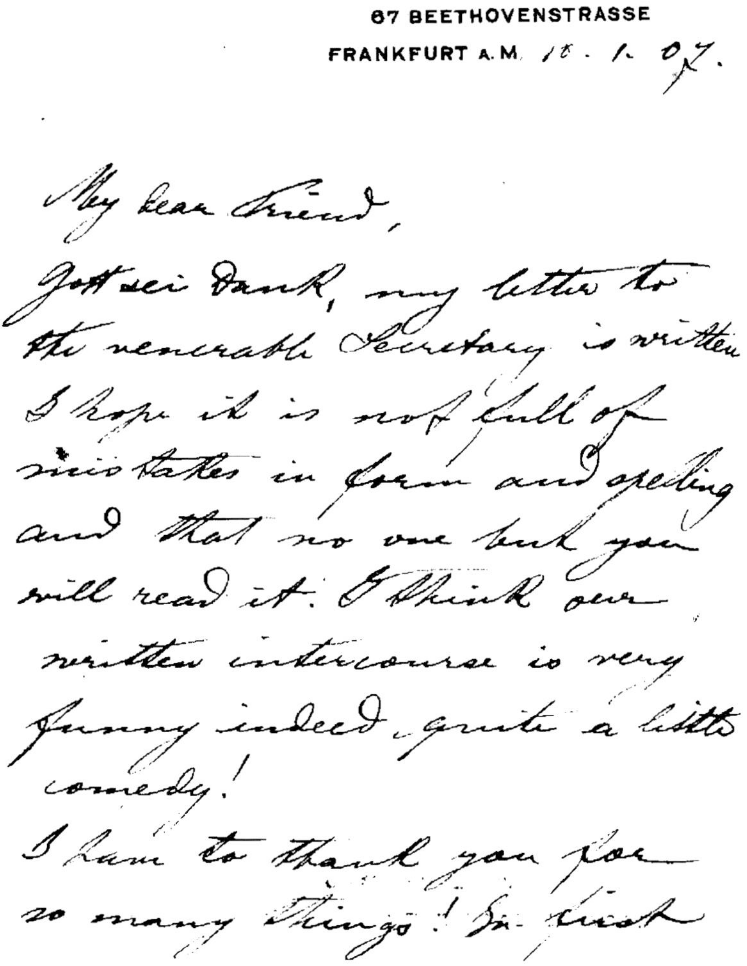

67 BEETHOVENSTRASSE
FRANKFURT A.M. 10. 1. 07.

My dear Friend,

Gott sei Dank, my letter to the venerable Secretary is written. I hope it is not full of mistakes in form and spelling and that no one but you will read it. I think our written intercourse is very funny indeed, quite a little comedy!

I have to thank you for so many things! In first

Plate 5 Letter from Constance Schweich to Israel Gollancz of 10 January 1907.

Plate 6 Painting of Constance Goetze (née Schweich) in Florentine dress, by Sigismund Goetze (1911).

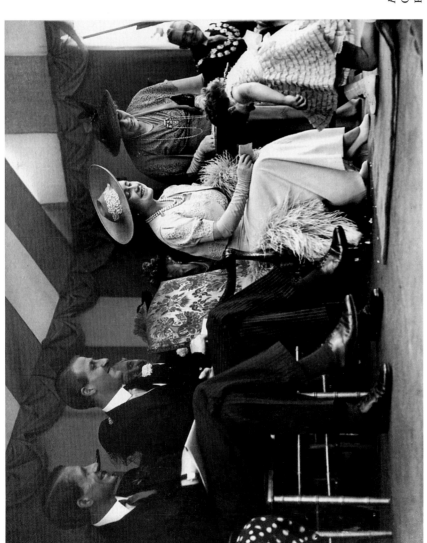

Plate 7 Constance Goetze with Queen Elizabeth at Grove House, Regent's Park, July 1939.

Plate 8 The 'Triton' Fountain in Queen Mary's Garden, Regent's Park (1950), paid for from the Constance Fund.

more interesting letters and offering-lists discovered later, Sayce found plenty of biblical interest to write about in his introduction and, rather prematurely, concluded that this new evidence supported the existence of monotheistic belief at Elephantine. In other words, at the very time when the Schweich bequest was being made, Mond was in direct contact with Sayce about a discovery which was already perceived to be of considerable biblical interest (and which was to be the subject of the Schweich Lectures in 1914). Mond presented a copy of the volume to the Society of Biblical Archaeology, of which Sayce had been the President since 1898, and became a member in November 1907.[37] One might indeed wonder whether the requirement in the Schweich Trust Deed, which followed closely the terms proposed by the donor, that 'all scholars of whatsoever School of thought' should be eligible for appointment was originally intended to ensure that, in this highly controversial field, conservatives like Sayce should be chosen to lecture as well as mainstream Old Testament scholars like S. R. Driver. If so, it was only successful in a small way: Sayce never gave the Schweich Lectures and the only real conservative to do so in the early years was E. Naville in 1915.[38]

---

37 *Proceedings of the Society of Biblical Archaeology* 1907, p. 252.
38 One further item may be connected with the Schweich family. Help from a 'Leopold-Schweich-Stiftung' is acknowledged by a German scientist writing in 1933 (see *Annalen der Physik* 408/1 [1933], 38). Might this have been Emile's memorial to his father? His obituary speaks of his 'many benefactions' but does not mention this one.

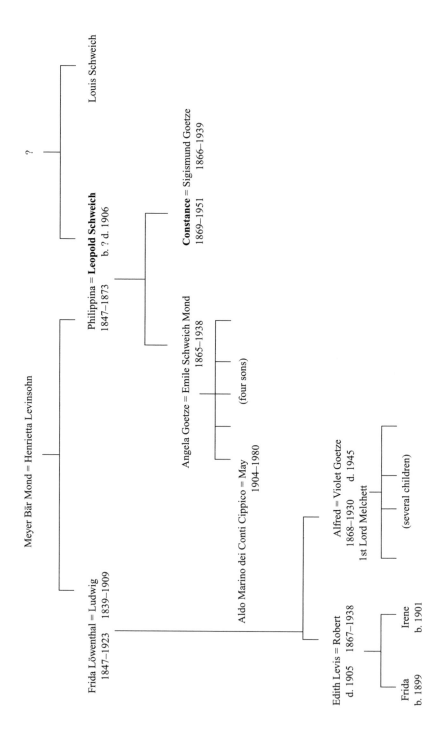

Meyer Bär Mond = Henrietta Levinsohn

?

Louis Schweich

Philippina = **Leopold Schweich**
1847–1873   b. ? d. 1906

Frida Löwenthal = Ludwig
1847–1923   1839–1909

Constance = Sigismund Goetze
1869–1951   1866–1939

Angela Goetze = Emile Schweich Mond
1865–1938

(four sons)

Aldo Marino dei Conti Cippico = May
1904–1980

Alfred = Violet Goetze   d. 1945
1868–1930
1st Lord Melchett

(several children)

Edith Levis = Robert
d. 1905   1867–1938

Frida
b. 1899

Irene
b. 1901

Figure 1 The Family of Leopold and Constance Schweich.

APPENDIX 1

Letters from Constance Schweich to Israel Gollancz

1. Constance Schweich to Israel Gollancz, 10 January 1907
(Sir Israel Gollancz Correspondence, Manuscripts Division, Department of Rare
Books and Special Collections, Princeton University Library, 3/12)

67 Beethovenstrasse
Frankfurt a.M. 10.1.07

My dear Friend,

Gott sei Dank, my letter to the venerable Secretary is written.[1] I hope it is not
full of mistakes in form and spelling and that no one but you will read it. I think
our written intercourse is very funny indeed, quite a little comedy!

I have to thank you for so many things! In first line for all the trouble you took
and are still taking for the Memorial, and your great kindness in fulfilling all my
wishes in connection with it.[2]

2. For your kind letters and good wishes and last, not least, for the charming little
book you sent me. It is so pretty, I read the dainty rhymes with great pleasure.

I was so glad that you went to Paris with my darling auntie[3] and poor Robert.[4]
My thoughts were permanently with them during the sad days, which ought to
be days of joy for all![5] I am sure your sympathy and friendship was a great help
and that the little ones were more than happy with you. Irene[6] is a great favourite
of mine, she is most original and such a sensitive, warm-hearted little creature.
Both children are of a sweet disposition and want love and devotion. Let us hope
life will be kind to them and compensate their cruel loss.[7]

---

1 The 'venerable Secretary' is Gollancz himself, who was Secretary of the British Academy
   from its foundation in 1902 until his death in 1930. The letter probably related to the
   Leopold Schweich Fund, about which there had already been correspondence in October
   1906. On the drawn-out process at the Academy see Chapter 2, pp. 16–21.
2 The 'Memorial' will be the Fund to be set up in memory of Leopold Schweich, which
   was referred to as a 'memorial' in the Academy's announcement.
3 Mrs Frida Mond.
4 Robert (later Sir Robert) Mond: see above, pp. 9–11.
5 Probably a reference to the Christmas season, during which the visit had taken place.
6 Robert and Edith Mond's younger daughter, born in 1901; the elder daughter, Fri(e)da,
   was born in 1899.
7 The death of their mother in 1905, probably in December, which would explain the 'sad
   days' above as meaning the first anniversary of her death—Cohen, *Life*, pp. 235–6, and
   Goodman, *Mond Legacy*, p. 78, place it at the beginning of 'a winter holiday' (of Ludwig
   and Frida Mond).

I half thought you would perhaps come to Frankfurt from Paris. But the weather was so bitterly cold that I am glad you did not come, especially as you had so little time to stay. Besides two friends, one of Bonn, one of Würzburg, both teachers, were my guests and I had to take them out a good deal.—Since my return I had constantly visitors and my work suffered by these permanent interruptions—I neglected my music sadly and began to practice seriously only a few days ago.[8]

The lectures I hear are most interesting, especially:

French Literature, by Morf.[9]
With Prof. Curtis[10], we are reading Byron—Caïn just now—
I take Italian lessons and read: il Paradiso, di Dante.
Then I hear one lecture on Frederic the Great and take a practical course of experimental Psychology.

—If you add to my 11 lectures household and society duties, theatres and concerts, you will understand that I am writing to you at 1 o'clock in the morning. Everyone is in bed, only both my doggies are sleeping at my side. They look up, now and then, just to warn me that it is time to rest. And I shall obey,

Good night—or good morning—just as you like—I wish you both and many, many happy days.

> Very truly yours,
> Constance Schweich

8 On Constance's later musical performances see above, p. 7.
9 This will be Heinrich Morf, whose planned *Geschichte der neuern französischen Literatur (XVI.–XIX. Jahrhundert)* in four volumes did not get beyond the first: *Das Zeitalter der Renaissance* (Strassburg, K. J. Trübner, 1898; 2nd edn 1914). He was a Professor at the newly established Akademie für Sozial- und Handelswissenschaft at Frankfurt (the University of Frankfurt was only founded in 1914) from 1901 to 1910 and its first Rector from 1901 to 1903 (*NDB* 18, pp. 100–2). The Akademie was presumably the venue for this and the other lectures mentioned.
10 A Fr Curtis was Professor of Englische Philologie at the time of the conversion of the Akademie into the University of Frankfurt in 1914, and he is probably the F. J. Curtis who was one of the editors of the Festschrift for the *Neuphilologentag* held in Frankfurt in 1912, to which he contributed an essay on a sixteenth-century English–French phrase-book.

2. Constance Schweich to Israel Gollancz, 29 March 1907 (a correspondence card)
(Sir Israel Gollancz Correspondence, Manuscripts Division, Department of Rare
Books and Special Collections, Princeton University Library, 3/12)

C.S.   67 Beethovenstrasse

Frankfurt a.M. 29.3[11].07

Dear Friend,

I hope the official answer is what you want. It seems to me that the Declaration
of Trust[12] could not be better and I thank you once more for all the trouble it
gave you. I do hope that you will take a good rest during the holidays, you must
be quite overworked. I am leaving for Cannes on Monday, Hotel Gallia, where
I beg to address your next letter. It would be jolly to meet there. I shall stay
till ab.[out] 12th of April. Dear little Frida[13] seems to be much better, I am so
dreadfully sad that poor Mrs[?] Mond[14] had to suffer so much anxiety. She has
so little sunshine in her life and wants it so much.

    Auf Wiedersehen! Yours very sincerely
    Constance Schweich

11 The numeral is not quite clear—it could be a '9'—but the reference to staying until 12
     April makes March the most likely month, and this would also fit in with Gollancz's
     'holidays' from his university duties.
12 The official document establishing the Leopold Schweich Fund. Evidence from the
     British Academy archives shows that this had been prepared and given broad approval
     by the Council already in January 1907, but that discussion of details in a sub-committee
     was continuing in February. Final approval was not given until later in the year (see
     Chapter 2, p. 21). The indication of Constance's approval here will be the basis for
     Gollancz's statement in a letter to Sir Spencer Walpole of 6.4.1907 (also in the Academy
     archives) that 'my friend. . .quite approves of the Scheme embodied in the Declaration
     of Trust'. The same letter implies ('I have now at the bank') that the actual donation of
     £10,000 had only very recently reached Gollancz.
13 Presumably Robert Mond's elder daughter: see above, n. 6.
14 Most likely the elder Frida Mond, wife of Ludwig Mond, with whom Gollancz was often
     in close contact. Her tendency to depression and her need for supportive company earlier
     in her life is mentioned by Rischbieter, *Henriette Hertz*, pp. 50–1.

Chapter 2

The Schweich Lectures

The Beginnings

THE FIRST SERIES OF SCHWEICH LECTURES were delivered in the spring of 1908 by Canon S. R. Driver, Regius Professor of Hebrew at Oxford and one of the founding Fellows of the British Academy.[1] But the process which led to this began some eighteen months earlier, when at a Council meeting on 31 October 1906 the Secretary of the Academy, Israel Gollancz, read out a letter dated 10 October offering a gift of £10,000 'for the furtherance of research in the Archaeology and art, the history, languages, and literature of Ancient Civilization, with reference to Biblical Archaeology'.[2] As already mentioned, the letter is unfortunately no longer where it was pasted in the minute-book, but the minutes record that it was accompanied by 'proposed rules and regulations'. What these rules and regulations were can to some extent be inferred from a manuscript document in the hand of Gollancz, unfortunately not dated, headed 'Munificent Gift to the British Academy'.[3] This looks like the text for the public announcement of the gift, which was to be made on 15 January 1907 and then at a General Meeting of the Academy on 30 January, and it seems also to have served as a press release.[4]

---

1   To be precise, on 18 and 30 March and 2 April at Burlington House: *The Times* 20.3.1908, p. 19, and 3.4.1908, p. 17, with summaries of the lectures.
2   Council Minute-Book, 1902–7.
3   File '1907', in British Academy (BA) archives, (Gollancz) BA Papers and Correspondence 1903–9. See also the President's address at the AGM later in the year, *Proceedings of the British Academy* 3 (1907–8), pp. 2–3.
4   *The Times* 15.1.1907, p. 8. See also the announcements in *Nature* 75 (1906–7), p. 278, and *American Anthropologist*, NS 9/1 (1907), p. 241, which reproduce (almost) the precise wording of the first half of the document, except for (in the latter case) the amount of the gift, which is mistakenly said to be £100,000. The wording is very close to parts of the draft Deed mentioned below.

The document speaks more broadly of 'Biblical Study' as the special point of reference for the research to be supported by the Fund, which was to be named after 'the late Mr. Leopold Schweich of Paris'. The donor was originally not publicly named, but the Council minutes indicate that it was Leopold Schweich's daughter Constance, and this has been stated in the Academy's publications for some time. Her gift seems not to have come out of the blue, as a letter in the archives from Gollancz to another Fellow of the Academy describes her as 'my friend'.[5]

The procedure for the formal acceptance of this gift and the legal establishment of the Fund extended over more than a year. At first progress was rapid. Council appointed a sub-committee to oversee matters (Gollancz, E. M. Thompson, C. G. Ilbert and J. Armitage Robinson) and its first task was to approve the regulations proposed in principle. It was then agreed to have a Deed of Trust embodying the donor's proposals drawn up by a solicitor: this was presented to the next meeting of Council and referred back to the sub-committee for comment, with a provision for them to add any regulations which they thought fit.[6] A copy was presumably sent to Constance Schweich and her 'letter to the venerable Secretary' referred to in her letter to Gollancz of 10 January 1907 (see the Appendix to Chapter 1) may well have indicated her approval of it. Three copies of the draft survive in the Academy's archives, and two of them have annotations proposing changes in the wording, many of which found their way into the final version.[7] Although they are not dated, there is good reason to see these copies as earlier than the discussions which took place in February 1907 (below) and the fact that their printed text coincides very closely with that of the public announcement mentioned above implies that it is what the Academy's solicitor had provided for the Council meeting on 12 December 1906. The annotations on one copy show considerable impatience with some of the legal terminology: 'There is no magic or even utility in "said"' (as in 'the said trust fund'). The same writer also insisted that 'articles' (as

5 6.4.1907, to Sir Spencer Walpole, in 'Papers and Correspondence 1907': cf. *Proceedings of the British Academy* 3 (1907–8), p. 2. Gollancz's skill as a fund-raiser for the Academy, and also for King's College London, is recalled in his obituary (by F. G. Kenyon) in *Proceedings of the British Academy* 16 (1930), pp. 431–2, and in Kenyon, *First Fifty Years*, pp. 17–18—here, perhaps significantly a year after her death, Constance Schweich is explicitly named as the donor.

6 Council Minutes, 28.11.1906 and 12.12.1906.

7 See 'Papers and Correspondence 1907'.

obtained by excavators) should be replaced by 'objects', because '"articles" savours too much of the retail trade'.

At a meeting of Council on 30 January (before the General Meeting) the draft Deed was discussed again, agreed in principle and the President was authorised to seal it.[8] But some problems of drafting must have surfaced at or after the meeting, as can be seen from letters sent to Gollancz during February by the other members of the sub-committee.[9] They were concerned about two paragraphs (§§ 12 and 13) that dealt with the ownership and disposal of objects discovered in the course of any excavations that might be supported from the Fund. It is possible to reconstruct the progress of the argument with some certainty by careful study of the letters. The initial point at issue was a proposal from Thompson to insert in § 13 a clause which included not only objects excavated but those obtained in other ways by excavators supported by the Fund. He writes (belatedly on 20 February— he had mislaid the document) of 'my suggestion': 'I had in mind the fact that excavators *obtain* antiq[uitie]s by other means as well as by excavation'. As the Director of the British Museum he had good reason to know.[10] Robinson began his letter (of 7 February) with this point and gave the suggestion his strong support: 'We ought therefore to insert the words, if we retain Clause 12, or a false distinction might seem to arise'. Ilbert, in a brief note sent on the following day, was not convinced: 'I think it would be going too far to insert the words "or obtained" in § 13'. He was himself a lawyer, who had specialised in drafting trusts early in his career and was highly regarded as a parliamentary draftsman and an expert on constitutional law, and the weight of his authority seems to have decided the matter: the words are not included in the final version of § 13.[11] Thompson, in his letter, had noted the disagreement (Gollancz evidently reported the others' views to him) and said that he would like to see Gollancz to find a way of resolving it. Robinson had more success with some proposals of his own to amend § 12. The earlier discussion of the draft had left the paragraph in a state which he saw as 'ambiguous or confusing', because it seemed to him to

8   Council Minutes, 30.1.1907. One reason for delay emerges from these minutes (and those of 27 February): the Academy did not yet possess a seal of its own, and only now were steps being taken to design and make one!

9   'Papers and Correspondence 1907'.

10 The initial announcement of the gift had been broadly phrased: 'any article...obtained by excavators'.

11 On Ilbert see *Oxford Dictionary of National Biography* 29, pp. 194–5.

differentiate between excavated objects, which belonged to the Academy, and other 'objects of interest' which were to be offered as a gift to the British Museum. Robinson, who was not only Dean of Westminster but an expert on the interpretation of biblical texts, therefore proposed some neat transpositions of key phrases in the draft which would remove the problem. Thompson was not so sure that the changes were needed, but they were incorporated into the document that was eventually enacted.

Once agreement had been reached, Gollancz must have sent a copy of the revised text to Constance Schweich, and it will be to this that she refers in her card of 29 March when she says: 'It seems to me that the Declaration of Trust could not be better'. The 'trouble' for Gollancz which she goes on to mention will certainly have included the handling of the sub-committee. She also says that she hopes that 'the official answer is what you want'. This probably meant the (renewed) approval of Council.

At about the same time it appears that the £10,000 had reached the Academy's bank account: on 6 April Gollancz was writing to Sir Spencer Walpole, a Fellow of the Academy and a member of the Council, to seek advice about how to invest it: 'I now have at the Bank the £10,000 from my friend', and he takes the opportunity to add: 'who quite approves of the Scheme embodied in the Declaration of Trust'.[12] He asks Walpole to consult 'the Agent of the Bank of England' for advice about both investments and procedure. Walpole was a historian, but he had also been the Governor of the Isle of Man, Secretary of the Post Office and active recently in business, including the London, Brighton and South Coast Railway.[13] The advice was evidently secured, Council approved the investment of the money at its meeting on 1 May and some further details at the meeting on 15 May. A month later, at the Annual General Meeting on 11 June, the President, Lord Reay, reported that half the sum was in Bank of England Stock and half in 'the 3½ per cent Inscribed Stock of the Government of New South Wales'.[14]

The meeting of 1 May also agreed the membership of a committee to oversee the activities to be financed by the Schweich fund: the members now included the biblical scholars Robinson, W. Sanday and F. C. Burkitt, but also the President, Ilbert and Gollancz himself as Secretary. The new

---

12 'Papers and Correspondence 1907'.
13 *Oxford Dictionary of National Biography* 57, pp. 93–94; cf. *Proceedings of the British Academy* 3 (1907–8), p. 8 ('his experience in business').
14 *Proceedings of the British Academy* 3 (1907–8), p. 2.

committee met, apparently for the first time, on 19 June.[15] It agreed to recommend S. R. Driver to the Council as the first Schweich Lecturer, proposing as the subject 'the results of archaeological research as bearing on the Study of the Old Testament', with the intention that it should be 'of the nature of an Introductory Course, giving the lead to the work of the Fund'. This recommendation was approved by the Council when it met on 4 July. Gollancz did not wait for this and wrote to Driver on 24 June, hoping for an answer by 4 July.[16] Perhaps fortunately (in case some might have thought Gollancz over-hasty) Driver did not reply at once and needed a second letter to chase him up—to which he replied on a postcard stamped on 3 July that he had been mulling over the invitation because of his other commitments and his wish to consult his colleague Sanday. His promised reply, also dated 3 July, does not survive but it was affirmative and this was duly reported to Council on 25 July.[17]

In the meantime further problems had arisen about the Declaration of Trust. At the meeting of Council on 4 July two letters from a firm of solicitors (Messrs Lewis and Yglesias), dated 18 May and 1 July, 'as to the Execution of the Declaration of Trust of the Sc[h]weich Fund' were read out. The issue was serious and complex enough to require the appointment of yet another sub-committee, entirely separate (apart from the President, Gollancz and Ilbert) from the official Schweich Committee.[18] But what exactly the issue was remains obscure. It is not even clear whose solicitors Messrs Lewis and Yglesias were: were they acting for the Academy, or for someone else, and if so who? Could it have been Constance Schweich? There is a long letter to Gollancz from one of the new sub-committee members, T. E. Holland, which speaks of 'the need to extricate ourselves from a rather awkward position' and the proposals which he went on to make give some clues to what the problem was.[19] They begin with some general regulations

15 Schweich Committee Minutes 19.6.1907.
16 'Papers and Correspondence 1907'.
17 Council Minutes 25.7.1907.
18 Council Minutes 4.7.1907. The other members were Prof. T. E. Holland, Sir F. Pollock and Sir Spencer Walpole, but the last-named died suddenly on 7 July and was replaced by W. Anson (Council Minutes, 25.7.1907).
19 The letter, in 'Papers and Correspondence 1907', is dated 7 July 1907. The very precise references to 'clause' and line which Holland gives in it show that the copy of the document that he had is not the original one, but one in which revisions had already been entered. This is confirmed by the fact that he proposes to insert words in § 10 which are very similar to some that had been in the original version but were marked for deletion in one of the copies mentioned above. No copy of the version seen by Holland seems to survive.

for the use of the Academy's seal, requiring that it be kept under lock and key and that when it was used (by the President, or failing him the Secretary) two Fellows of the Academy should be present and witness the sealing by their signatures. Holland returned to the issue of procedure at the end of his letter, so it must have been important. Probably the solicitors had pointed out that the sealing of the Deed (if indeed it had been done) had not been done in the manner required by law. Holland went on to propose some fresh amendments to the Deed. Most of them are minor and not all of them were adopted. But his first amendments, which were adopted, were to parts of the preamble which dealt with the acceptance of the donation and it is likely these addressed criticisms that the revision of the Deed had not taken account of the actual receipt of the money and its investment. At any rate, although Holland himself did not mention the point specifically, care was taken in the final revision of § 1 to add a statement about where the money was now invested. At the Council meeting on 6 November there was a report from the new 'drafting' Committee, which had met on 22 October, recommending that 'the declaration of trust be prepared as a deed . . . and be duly stamped', and this was agreed, though not until some procedural amendments had been defeated.[20] The printed final version is dated 'November 6, 1907'.

This was the very first such benefaction to be received by the Academy since its foundation in 1902, and it came at a time when, despite vigorous lobbying, it did not yet receive any Government grant. The Academy's appreciation for the benefaction was all the greater because of its potential wider significance and this was eloquently expressed by Thompson in his Presidential Address in 1908:

> The moral value of a benefaction of this nature, when conferred, as this has been, upon a Society in the early years of its foundation, is hardly to be overestimated. Here is a recognition of the high position taken by the British Academy, and of its ability to dispense such benefactions in the best interests of learning. It is for this reason that we, the Fellows of one of the youngest Academies of the world, owe a debt of gratitude to the generous donor who has entrusted the Schweich Fund to our care.[21]

The clauses of the deed contain the usual statements about the origins of the Fund and its purpose (as in the donor's original letter [above, p. 16] except for the substitution of 'Biblical Study' for 'Biblical Archaeology' as the point of reference), as well as the procedures for its future management.

---

20 Council Minutes 6.11.1907; cf. *Proceedings of the British Academy* 3 (1907–8), p. 10 (AGM, June 1908).
21 *Proceedings of the British Academy* 3 (1907–8), p. 11.

The main clause (para. 5) makes it clear that only the income from the Fund's investments could be spent (but its use could be deferred to later years) and provides for three kinds of permitted expenditure. First, 'not less than three public lectures' were to be delivered annually on subjects coming within the expressed purpose of the Fund, for which a fee of fifty guineas was to be paid. Secondly, expenses connected with the lectures could be defrayed, including the cost of publication of the text of the lectures, which was to be delivered promptly by the lecturer and was to be held in copyright by the Academy. Thirdly, the remainder of the income each year should be applied 'primarily for the purposes of excavation in furtherance of the objects specified' as the purpose of the Fund. But it could also be used 'in the second place for the publication of the results of original research in connexion with one or more of such objects', and at the Council's discretion it could be allocated to other ways of furthering the purpose of the Fund. A later clause which, as we have seen, gave some trouble to the drafters (para. 12) took the support of excavations sufficiently seriously to assert the Academy's ownership of any 'objects of interest' obtained in the course of excavations and to direct that they should be offered as a gift to the British Museum or some other Museum in the United Kingdom (as long as local law permitted it). The aim of funding excavations was included in the first announcements about the Fund and evidently originated with the donor and her advisors. The income from the Fund (perhaps £300 per annum) could have been expected to leave a sizeable sum each year for such use, once expenditure on the lectures had been covered.

It was very probably this provision for the support of excavation which drew the interest of the Hon. Secretary of the Palestine Exploration Fund (PEF), J. D. Crace, who wrote to Gollancz on 7 February 1907 and was answered that his letter would be referred to the Council of the Academy.[22] The original letter seems not to have survived, but the PEF. was at this time in the midst of supporting R. A. S. Macalister's excavations at Gezer (1902–5, 1907–9) and was in serious need of additional funds.[23] However,

22 To J. D. Crace, 11.2.1907, 'Papers and Correspondence 1907'.
23 *Palestine Exploration Fund Quarterly Statement* (April) 1907, p. 82. It is probably no coincidence that the statement (which emphasised the contribution of the Gezer excavation to 'Biblical study') was placed immediately after a report of the Schweich benefaction—a 'handsome bequest'—and its intended uses, 'the comprehensive character of which provides numerous ways for the advantageous expenditure of the money devoted to it'.

the same sub-committee that recommended S. R. Driver as the first Schweich Lecturer also affirmed in June that 'the grant of financial assistance to outside enterprises cannot at present be considered', and Council agreed.[24] This was understandable enough, as the money had only just been invested and no income would yet have been received. There may also have been some uncertainty about what the costs associated with the lectures might be.

In selecting persons to lecture, or undertake other work, the Council was required by the Deed (para. 14) to consider 'women equally with men' and 'all scholars of whatsoever school of thought', worthy aims which, in the first case at least, seem to have been found more difficult to put into practice.

Despite its early reluctance to give grants from the Schweich Fund to support enterprises other than the lectures, the Academy did eventually make this a regular practice for a time. The first grants, in 1913, were made to the Egypt Exploration Fund for work at Abydos (£600) and to Dr A. Souter for work on Pelagius, but none are recorded for the following years. Only in 1918 did the then new President, F. G. Kenyon, note at the Annual General Meeting that the Fund

> has a considerable margin available for exploration and excavation in Bible lands. We hope that it will be possible to put this fund to the use for which it is specifically intended in the near future, when research in the Holy Land will be practicable under conditions more favourable than ever in the past.

Later in his address Kenyon made clear what he meant, reporting on the steps that were already being taken, at the Academy's initiative, for the setting up of the British School of Archaeology in Jerusalem, for which 'generous subscriptions' had already been received, and he even stated that the Schweich Fund had given the Academy a special reason for being interested in this project. It is not too difficult to discern something of the cooperation which was evidently going on between Kenyon and the Academy on the one hand and Robert Mond on the other (see above, Chapter 1, n. 35). The Palestine Exploration Fund was also involved. It is then not at all surprising to find that grants began to be given from the Schweich Fund to the Palestine Exploration Fund for work at Ascalon (Ashkelon), Gaza and Jerusalem (Ophel), as well as to the Egypt Exploration Society, in the early 1920s. A smaller sum was given for work on the Patristic Greek

24 Minutes of 4.7.1907.

Lexicon.[25] From 1925 the Academy was able to secure £2000 of research funds from the Government, but disbursements from the Schweich Fund, mainly for excavations, evidently continued through the 1920s and 1930s, and perhaps a little longer.[26]

The Lectures

In all sixty-seven series of Schweich Lectures have been given so far.[27] Sixty-six of these were given by men (one by a team of three, in 1926: as provided for in para. 8 of the Trust Deed), and only one by a woman (Kathleen Kenyon in 1963). The shortfall in the total number is due to the fact that in 1951 Council decided, for financial reasons, that the lectures should be biennial and in 1976 that they should be triennial, as they are now.[28] Those who possess, or have seen in a library, the full set of published volumes may be surprised that the total number is so high. Lists of the published volumes (for example, on the dust-jackets) could give the impression that there were numerous gaps, especially from the 1940s on. But thanks to the researches of James Rivington, the Academy's Publications Officer, we now have a complete list of all the lectures that were given, which appears as an Appendix to this chapter, and this shows that a regular sequence of lectures was maintained—the gaps in the list of published volumes being due mainly to defaulting authors, but in a few cases to Council's view that the text submitted was not up to the high standard required. The statistics that I shall give now are based on the full list.

On a purely personal level, two scholars have given the lectures twice, as also permitted by para. 8 (R. H. Kennett in 1909 and 1931; F. C. Burkitt in 1913 and 1926, in the latter case only one of the three lectures). There have been three cases of a father and son, or in one case a daughter, giving the lectures: the best known will be the Drivers in 1908 and 1944, but there

---

25 *Proceedings of the British Academy* 6 (1913–14), p. 5; 8 (1917–18), pp. 44, 48–9, 53–4; 10 (1921–2), pp. 17, 21, 27; 11 (1924–5), pp. 4–5.
26 See the summary of 'Grants from the Schweich and Henriette Hertz Funds' given by Kenyon, in *Fifty Years*, p. 29.
27 A series on the modern study of the Latin Bible was to have been given by Dom B. Fischer in 1981, but he had to withdraw because of illness. This made it possible to have lectures in two successive years in 1983 and 1984.
28 Minutes 23.5.1951, 19.12.1976.

were also the Kenyons in 1932 and 1963 and the Sukenik/Yadins in 1930 and 1970 (the latter a very biblical generational gap!). Some volumes have been reprinted several times, notably those by S. R. Driver (1908), H. H Rowley (1948), E. Ullendorff (1967) and D. J. Wiseman (1985); and others have appeared in a revised edition (St John Thackeray [1920], Kahle [1941], de Vaux [1959]), or even two (G. R. Driver [1944]). In one case, de Vaux's lectures on Qumran, the opportunity of revision was taken to translate his original French text into English. According to Kathleen Kenyon's Foreword to the revised edition de Vaux actually gave his lectures in English, 'with occasional engaging mispronunciations at which he would laugh as well as anyone', and so he did not take advantage (as some others did) of the provision in the regulations (para. 10) that 'in very special circumstances the Council shall have power. . .to allow a Lecture to be given in a foreign language'. The only other series to be published in a foreign language were those of Van Hoonacker (1914), but the titles of those given by Dossin (1949), Puech (1957) and Parrot (1974), but not published, are also in French, and it seems that all of them were delivered in French.[29]

Not surprisingly the majority of the lectures have been given by British scholars (48). Of the rest the largest contingent were the French (7, six of them between 1949 and 1974, when they accounted for nearly half the lectures given). Four lecturers were from Germany; three from Israel (I include Sukenik even though the State of Israel did not yet exist when he gave his lectures); one each from Denmark, Switzerland and Belgium; and just two from the United States, in fact the last two lecturers at the time of writing. Perhaps the cost of bringing a scholar across the Atlantic was felt to be an obstacle in the past, but it remains surprising in view of the popularity of the subject of the lectures in America. The result, in any case, is that the lectures given over the past hundred years are very largely representative of European, and mainly British, approaches to their subject matter.

If we consider the disciplines in which the lecturers were specialists (which occasionally does not correspond to the subjects on which they lectured), the results are approximately as follows—I say 'approximately' because of the difficulty of categorising some scholars in the simple terms that are necessary for this kind of survey. The largest group, twenty-three,

---

29 See Council Minutes of 22.5.1957 and letters in the Schweich Committee files of 3.3.1971 and 6.10.1972.

were biblical scholars, nearly three-quarters of them specialising in the Old Testament rather than the New. Another five straddled Biblical Studies and Oriental Languages, most again with a leaning towards the Old Testament rather than the New. Twelve could be described as archaeologists, but the line between them and the Assyriologists (10) and the Egyptologists (3) can be especially difficult to draw. Another five were predominantly specialists in other Oriental languages. Smaller groups came from Rabbinics (3), Classics (3), Qumran Studies (2) and Patristics (1). If we then distinguish between the first half of the list (1908–1941) and the second half (1942–2007), we find that in the earlier years the proportion of biblical scholars was much higher than in the later years: indeed out of the first twenty series of lectures eleven were given by biblical scholars, while between 1951 and 1984 none were (if only the published lectures are counted the 'gap' begins after 1948). This latter feature is especially striking because it corresponds to the heyday of 'Biblical Archaeology': so, whatever may have been the case in other parts of the world, the Schweich Lectures were not at that time a vehicle for the domination of archaeologists by biblical scholars. If there was such a time in Britain, it would have been earlier.

The subjects dealt with in the lectures have covered a wider range than might at first sight have seemed likely. The back of the dust-jackets of the published volumes (though not their title-pages, which have simply 'The Schweich Lectures' in accordance with para. 7 of the Deed) for many years carried the heading 'The Schweich Lectures on Biblical Archaeology'. To judge from the copies in the Academy library, this practice began in 1921, with the publication of H. St J. Thackeray's lectures, and accompanied a redesign of the list of earlier lecturers, which added the number in the sequence, titles, degrees and other honours of the lecturers and the date of the lectures' delivery. The previous volume, published in 1920, had none of these features. 'Biblical Archaeology' remained on the outside of the dust-jacket until 1989, and reappeared on the inside in 2003. The change in 1921 can be associated with the new prominence which it was planned to give to excavation with the establishment of the British School of Archaeology shortly before, and perhaps specifically with F. G. Kenyon's interest in this project and the role of the Schweich Fund in it: his Presidency lasted until 1921. But it was not a complete innovation by any means. We have seen that the phrase was used in the first mentions of the Schweich Fund in Council Minutes, and it also appeared in the headlines of the *Times* reports of the first series of lectures in 1908. Subsequently it occurs in

Plate 9 S. R. Driver.

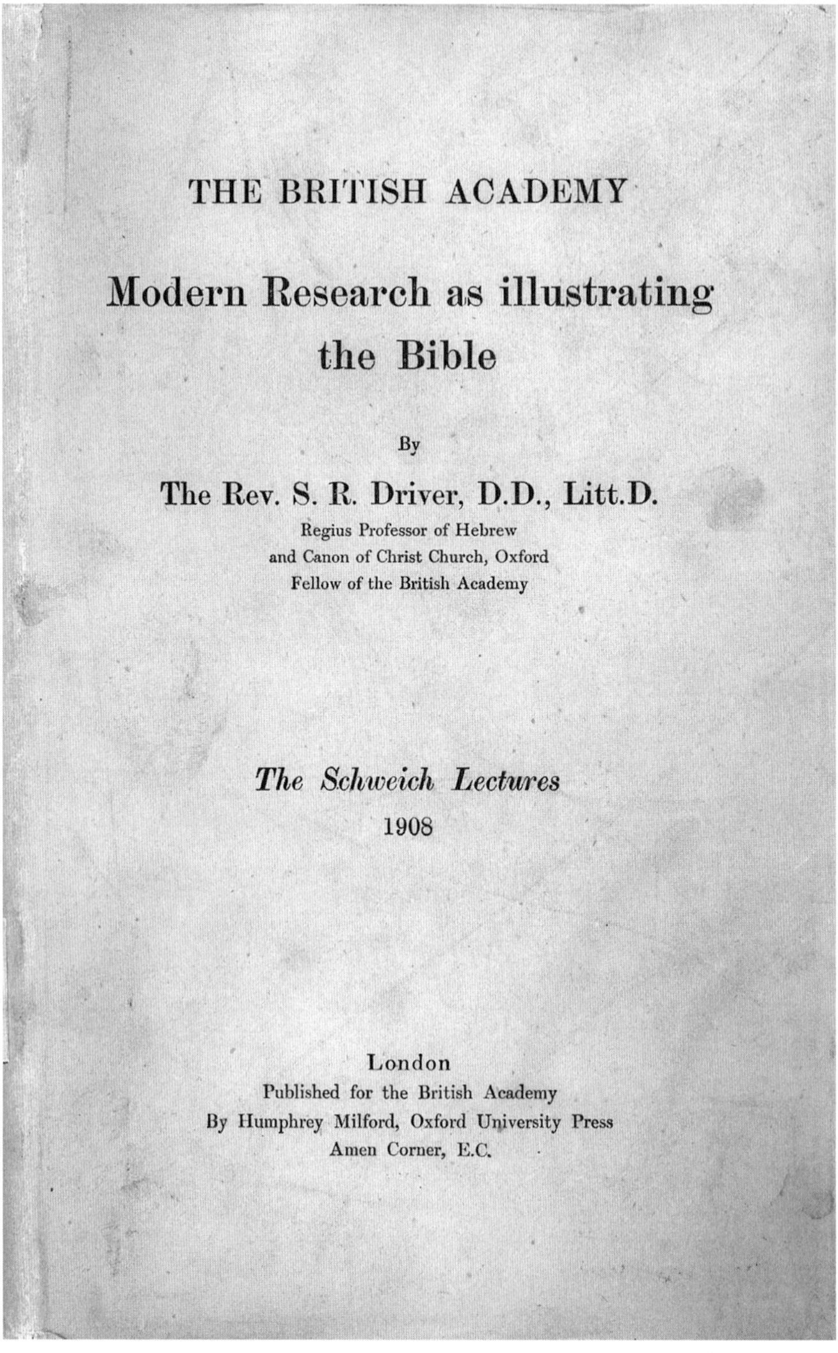

THE BRITISH ACADEMY

Modern Research as illustrating
the Bible

By

The Rev. S. R. Driver, D.D., Litt.D.

Regius Professor of Hebrew
and Canon of Christ Church, Oxford
Fellow of the British Academy

The Schweich Lectures

1908

London
Published for the British Academy
By Humphrey Milford, Oxford University Press
Amen Corner, E.C.

Plate 10 Dust jacket of the first Schweich Lectures, delivered by S. R. Driver in 1908, published in 1909 and reprinted six times (this is the 1922 impression).

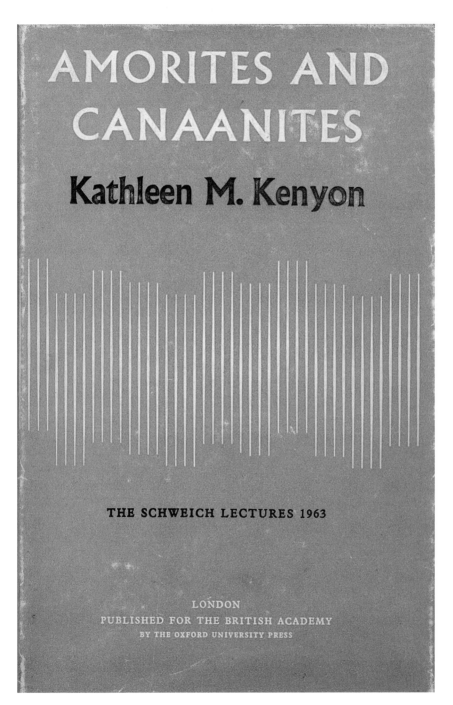

Plate 11 Kathleen Kenyon is the only woman to have delivered the Schweich Lectures – in 1963, published in 1966. At this point more ambitious jacket designs were introduced.

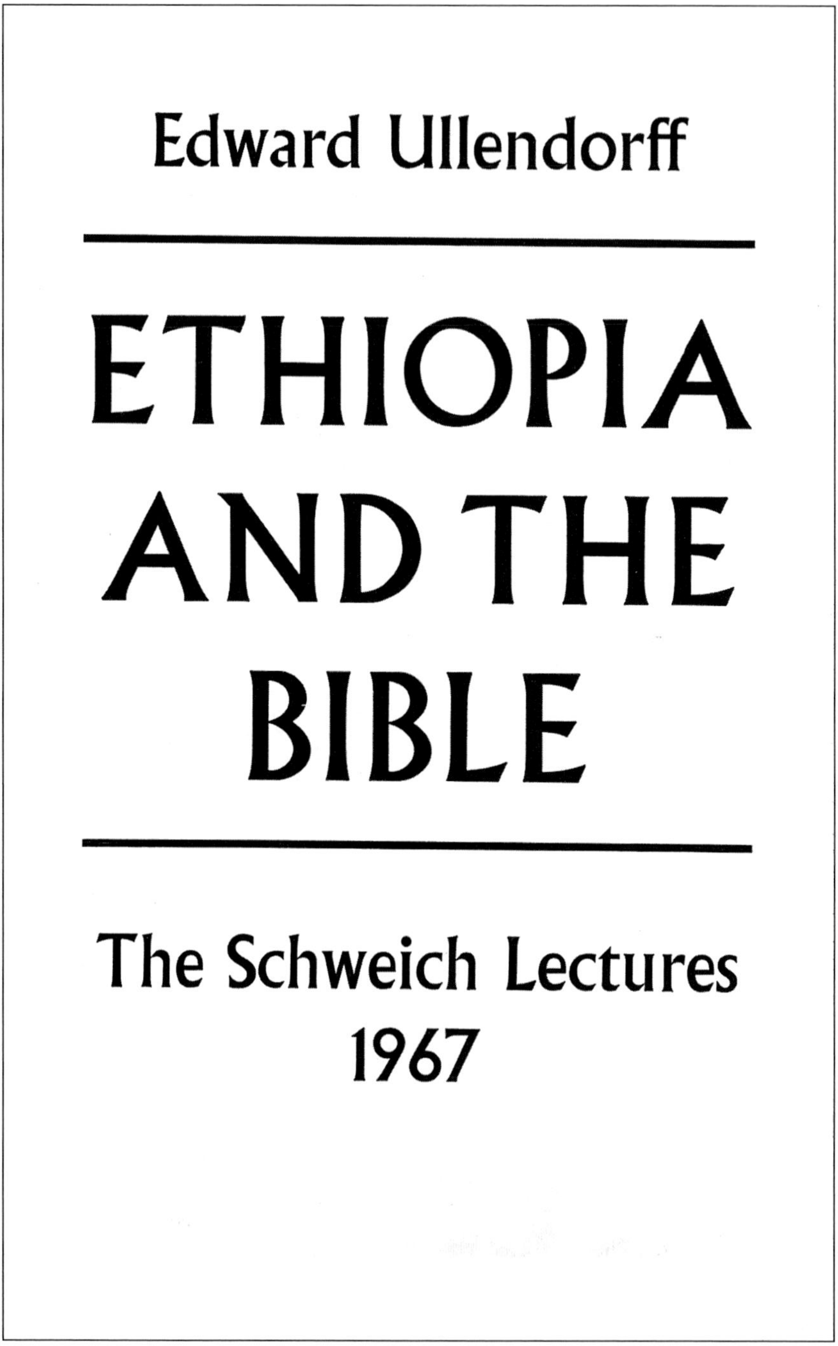

Edward Ullendorff

ETHIOPIA AND THE BIBLE

The Schweich Lectures 1967

Plate 12 Edward Ullendorff's lectures of 1967 have remained continuously in print since 1968; a paperback edition was published in 1988.

Presidential Addresses in 1910, 1911 and 1912, and then again from 1916,[30] although phrases that more clearly carried a broader meaning, like 'Biblical Study' and 'Biblical Research' were being used in the Academy's own documents from early in 1907.[31] The expression 'Biblical Archaeology' (which may conceivably have derived from the benefactor herself) was probably intended in these early years to carry the very wide sense which had been established over thirty-five years by the activities and publications of the 'Society for Biblical Archaeology', founded in 1871 and still active until 1918, which covered all kinds of investigation of what it is now customary to call 'the ancient Near East', often without any specific connection with the Bible.[32] In any case the Trust Deed is absolutely clear: although the 'Archaeology (. . .of Ancient Civilization)' is the first topic to be mentioned, it is followed by 'art, history, languages and literature'. The inclusion of non-archaeological topics as subjects for the lectures, both in the early days and more recently, is therefore entirely justified. Since I shall say more about the archaeological topics (conceived in a broad sense, as I will explain) in the next chapter, I will limit myself here to a brief outline of the others that have been treated. In all I count twenty-four such series, slightly more (14) in the first half of the sequence than the second. But whereas they appeared at fairly regular intervals until 1951, there was then a gap of sixteen years until the next non-archaeological series in 1967. By contrast between 1977 and 1995 there were five non-archaeological series and only two archaeological. Since 1995 all the topics have been archaeological.[33]

30 *Proceedings of the British Academy* 4 (1909–10), p. 14; 5 (1911–12), pp. 4, 12; 7 (1915–16), p. 19; 8 (1917–18), pp. 34, 44.
31 Council Minutes 30.1.1907; Presidential Addresses for 1907 and 1908 (*Proceedings of the British Academy* 3 [1907–8], pp. 2, 10).
32 See, e.g., the inaugural lecture of the Society by Samuel Birch, 'The Progress of Biblical Archaeology', published in *Transactions of the Society of Biblical Archaeology* 1 (1872), 1–12, and the use of the word 'Biblical' in the rules primarily as a geographical term. I am preparing a short study of the Society for publication: none of any extent appears to exist elsewhere.
33 It would of course be interesting to consider more fully the reasons for the balance of disciplines represented, their variation through time and the resulting impact of the lectures. No doubt both wider intellectual factors and the influence of individuals in the Academy and especially the Schweich Committee played a part in determining the way in which their purpose was conceived from time to time and the kind of people that it was thought appropriate to invite to lecture. A list of the members of the Schweich Committee would be a useful start for such a task.

A number of the non-archaeological series fall clearly under headings in the Trust Deed. Thus there were (1) three series on the Bible in Art, appropriately one each on Jewish, Christian and Islamic Art:

1927	James
1928	Arnold
1939	Leveen

(2) History appears once alone and once, in the very next year, with Literature:

1922	Abrahams
1923	Gaster

There have been more treatments of (3) the Bible in relation to various ancient languages and literatures, categories which it is difficult to separate:

1910	Smith (with reference to pre-Islamic Arab poetry)
1921	Margoliouth
1923	Gaster (in part)
1942	Knox
1967	Ullendorff (in part)
1992	Chadwick

With these we can perhaps include Naville's curious lectures of 1915, which argued, in a deliberately hostile response to biblical criticism, that the Old Testament had originally been written in cuneiform and was translated into Hebrew only at the time of the Babylonian Exile. This might be seen as a sign of respect for the requirement that 'all scholars of whatsoever school of thought' should be eligible to lecture, though the Council could reasonably have expected that Naville, who was a well known Egyptologist, would have chosen to lecture on a subject closer to his real expertise!

There remain two groups of topics which it is more difficult to place under any of the specific headings prescribed. A number dealt with (4) the Bible itself or closely related literature in various ways that did not involve comparison with other ancient civilisations, or only marginally so: these were mainly in the earlier period of the lectures:

1913	Burkitt
1919	Charles
1931	Kennett
1938	Welch
1943	Stevenson

A larger group dealt (5) with the textual criticism of the Bible, either in its original languages or in the ancient translations: this, though present in the early days, is more characteristic of recent times:[34]

1920	Thackeray
1932	Kenyon
1946	Zuntz
1951	Kilpatrick
1967	Ullendorff (in part)
1977	Roberts
1986	Barr
1989	Brock
1995	Knibb

From this brief survey it will already be clear what a varied contribution to the understanding of the Bible in its ancient context has been made by the Schweich Lecturers over the past century. Happy are those who possess, or have access to, the full set of published volumes, even if some of them are showing their age!

---

34 I could well have included Kahle's 1941 series here, but I have chosen to regard the finds from the Cairo Geniza as an archaeological discovery.

APPENDIX 2: THE TRUST DEED

(final form, as approved on 6 November 1907)

THE LEOPOLD SCHWEICH FUND

DECLARATION OF TRUST

TO ALL TO WHOM THESE PRESENTS SHALL COME THE BRITISH ACADEMY for the PROMOTION of HISTORICAL PHILOSOPHICAL and PHILOLOGICAL STUDIES (hereinafter called 'the Academy') SENDS GREETING.

WHEREAS the Academy was incorporated by Royal Charter dated the 8th day of August 1902 for the promotion of the study of the moral and political sciences including history philosophy law politics and economics archaeology and philology AND WHEREAS an offer was made to the Academy to pay unto the Academy the sum of ten thousand pounds for the purpose of establishing a Memorial to the late Leopold Schweich of Paris in the Republic of France Esquire deceased to be held by the Academy upon the trusts hereinafter expressed AND WHEREAS the Academy has agreed to accept the said sum and act as Trustee thereof accordingly and the said sum of ten thousand pounds has been paid to the account of the Academy at its Bankers (the receipt whereof the Academy hereby acknowledges) NOW THESE PRESENTS made in pursuance of the said agreement and in consideration of the premises WITNESS and the Academy hereby declares as follows:—

1. THE Academy will stand possessed of the said sum of ten thousand pounds now invested half in Bank of England Stock and half in the 3½% inscribed stock of the Government of New South Wales and all other sums which may hereafter be added thereto by gift bequest or otherwise UPON TRUST to invest the same in the name of the Academy in any of the investments from time to time by law authorised for the investment of trust funds with power from time to time to vary any such investments for other investments of a like authorised nature and the Academy will hold the said funds and the investments thereof (hereinafter called the trust fund) upon the trusts and for the purposes hereinafter declared.

2. The trust fund shall be called 'The Leopold Schweich Fund' and shall be dealt with under that name by a separate account in the books of the Academy.

3. The trust fund shall be devoted to the furtherance of research in the archaeology art history languages and literature of Ancient Civilization with reference to Biblical Study.

4. The control of the trust fund shall be vested in the Council of the Academy (hereinafter called 'the Council') who shall appoint a Committee for the purposes of the ordinary management thereof.

5. The income of the said trust fund shall be applied as follows:—

(a) The Council on the recommendation of the Committee as hereinafter provided shall procure not less than three public lectures to be delivered in every year dealing with some subject or subjects coming within the scope of the objects stated in Clause 3 hereof and the sum of fifty guineas shall be paid in each year out of the income of the said trust fund to or among the person or persons delivering such lecture or lectures.

(b) As soon as possible after the delivery of each lecture the lecturer shall deliver a written copy thereof to the Council in a form suitable for publication. The lecture and the copyright therein shall be the property of the Academy and the Council shall be the sole judges whether the lecture in whole or in part or any abstract thereof shall be published or not. Incidental expenses connected with any lecture including the expenses of publication and any translation which may be required shall be paid out of the income of the trust fund for the year in which the lecture shall be delivered.

(c) The residue of the income after the payments mentioned in sub-clauses *(a)* and *(b)* hereof in each year shall be applied primarily for the purposes of excavation in furtherance of one or more of the objects specified in Clause 3 of these presents and in the second place for the publication of the results of original research in connexion with one or more of such objects but it is declared that nothing herein contained shall fetter the discretion of the Council in case they shall think fit to apply such income for any other object specified in Clause 3 of these presents.

6. ANY surplus income which in any year the Council may not expend in any of the purposes aforesaid shall if the Council shall think fit be added to the capital of the trust fund but if the Council shall not think fit so to add the same they may apply such income in any subsequent year towards the purposes to which it would be applicable if it were income accruing in that year.

7. THE Lectures shall be called 'the Schweich Lectures'.

8. THE Council may appoint one person to deliver the whole of the Schweich Lectures in any one year or they may assign the lectures at their discretion to different persons. No person shall be appointed to deliver any Schweich Lecture in more years than three whether consecutive or not unless there shall be an interval of at least ten years between the last Schweich Lecture of such third year and the delivery by the same person of a Schweich Lecture or the first of a series of Schweich Lectures in a second or subsequent period of not more years than three as aforesaid.

9. THE Schweich Lectures shall be advertised and as the ordinary rule be delivered in London but in very special circumstances the Council shall have power if any reason appears to them to render such a course necessary to allow such Lectures to be delivered in any part of the United Kingdom of Great Britain and Ireland but in all circumstances at least one Schweich Lecture in the year shall be delivered in London.

10. EVERY Schweich Lecture shall be delivered in the English language and by the author of the Lecture. Provided that in very special circumstances the Council shall have power if any reason appears to them to render such a course necessary to allow a Lecture to be delivered in a foreign language or by a person not the author thereof but when any such lecture is delivered in a foreign language a translation thereof into English shall if the Council so require be supplied to the Council at least seven days before the delivery of the Lecture.

11. IN the case of any Schweich Lecture being delivered in a foreign language the Committee shall have the same rights powers and discretions with regard to the publication thereof or of the English translation thereof as with respect to a lecture delivered in the English language.

12. ALL objects obtained by excavations made in furtherance of the purposes specified in Clause 3 of these presents and any objects of interest connected with the aforesaid purposes which may be obtained by any excavator employed or paid out of the trust fund by the Council shall be the property of the Academy and shall subject to any provisions of the local law be offered in the first instance as a gift to the Trustees of the British Museum or if that class of objects be already in the opinion of the Council adequately represented in the British Museum then such objects shall be offered as a gift to some other museum in the United Kingdom.

13. BEFORE the final appointment or employment of any lecturer excavator or other person to do work for or on behalf of the Academy under the trusts hereof the Council shall procure every such person to enter into an agreement with the Academy binding himself to give effect to the provisions hereof so far as regards the ownership of and rights in any lecture delivered or objects excavated by such person.

14. IN selecting any person to lecture or to undertake excavation or travel or other work on behalf of the Academy in connexion with this trust the Council shall be free to appoint any person whether man or woman of any nationality and in making their choice the Council shall give equal consideration to all persons of whatsoever school of thought.

15. THE Committee which the Council shall appoint as hereinbefore provided shall consist of the President and Secretary of the Academy and of five other members to be from time to time elected by the Council who shall hold office for such period and shall retire in such order as the Council shall from time to time determine.

16. FOR the transaction of business a quorum of the Committee shall consist of three members.

17. AT all meetings of the Committee each question shall be decided by a majority of votes.

18. THE Council may appoint a member of the Committee to be chairman thereof and if no such chairman is appointed or if the chairman be not present then the Committee shall at each meeting appoint one of their number to take the chair at that meeting. The chairman of the meeting shall have one vote as a member of the Committee and in the event of equality of votes he shall also have a casting vote.

19. NO selection of the subject of a Schweich lecture or appointment of a lecturer or employment of an excavator or other person for the purposes specified in Clause 3 hereof and no application of the residue of income or any portion thereof shall be effectual or valid until the Committee shall have recommended such selection appointment employment or application to the Council at a meeting thereof and until the Council shall by resolution have approved such recommendation. If the Council reject any recommendation of the Committee they shall refer the matter back to the Committee for further consideration or for a fresh recommendation.

20. THE Council shall have power to make amend alter and repeal from time to time such further or other regulations as they shall think desirable for the due maintenance and administration of the said trust fund in furtherance of and consistent with the objects specified in Clause 3 of these presents.

21. IF any question shall arise as to the interpretation of any of the foregoing clauses, it shall be decided at a meeting of the Council by a majority of votes.

IN WITNESS whereof the British Academy have hereunto affixed their Common Seal this sixth day of November in the Year of Our Lord One Thousand Nine Hundred and Seven.

APPENDIX 3: SCHWEICH LECTURES

1908	S R Driver	*Modern Research as illustrating the Bible* (published 1909, reprinted 1909 [4 times], 1912, 1922)
1909	Robert H Kennett	*The Composition of the Book of Isaiah in the Light of History and Archaeology* (1910)
1910	George Adam Smith	*The Early Poetry of Israel in its Physical and Social Origins* (1912)
1911	R A Stewart Macalister	*The Philistines: Their History and Civilization* (1913)
1912	C H W Johns	*The Relations between the Laws of Babylonia and the Laws of the Hebrew Peoples* (1914)
1913	F Crawford Burkitt	*Jewish and Christian Apocalypses* (1914)
1914	A van Hoonacker	*Une Communauté Judéo-Araméenne à Éléphantine, en Égypte, aux VIe et Ve Siècles av. J.-C.* (1915)
1915	Édouard Naville	*The Text of the Old Testament* (1916)
1916	Leonard W King	*Legends of Babylon and Egypt in relation to Hebrew Tradition* (1918 [pbk], repr 1918 [hbk])
1917	C F Burney	*Israel's Settlement in Canaan: The Biblical Tradition and its Historical Background* (1918)
1918	A E Cowley	*The Hittites* (1920)
1919	R H Charles	*Lectures on the Apocalypse* (1922, repr 1923)
1920	H St John Thackeray	*The Septuagint and Jewish Worship: A Study in Origins* (1921; second edition 1923)
1921	D S Margoliouth	*The Relations between Arabs and Israelites prior to the Rise of Islam* (1924)
1922	Israel Abrahams	*Campaigns in Palestine from Alexander the Great* (1927)
1923	Moses Gaster	*The Samaritans: Their History, Doctrines and Literature* (1925)
1924	David George Hogarth	*Kings of the Hittites* (1926)
1925	Stanley A Cook	*The Religion of Ancient Palestine in the Light of Archaeology* (1930)
1926	Theodore H Robinson, J W Hunkin & F C Burkitt	*Palestine in General History* (1929)
1927	Montague Rhodes James	*The Apocalypse in Art* (1931)
1928	Thomas W Arnold	*The Old and New Testaments in Muslim Religious Art* (1932)
1929	T Eric Peet	*A Comparative Study of the Literatures of Egypt, Palestine, and Mesopotamia: Egypt's Contribution to the Literature of the Ancient World* (1931)
1930	E L Sukenik	*Ancient Synagogues in Palestine and Greece* (1934)
1931	R H Kennett	*Ancient Hebrew Social Life and Custom as Indicated in Law, Narrative and Metaphor* (1933)
1932	Frederic G Kenyon	*Recent Developments in the Textual Criticism of the Greek Bible* (1933)

1933	S Langdon	*Babylonian Menologies and the Semitic Calendars* (1935)
1934	Ernst E Herzfeld	*Archaeological History of Iran* (1935)
1935	S H Hooke	*The Origins of Early Semitic Ritual* (1938)
1936	Claude F A Schaeffer	*The Cuneiform Texts of Ras Shamra-Ugarit* (1939)
1937	J W Crowfoot	*Early Churches in Palestine* (1941)
1938	Adam C Welch	*The Work of the Chronicler: Its Purpose and its Date* (1939)
1939	Jacob Leveen	*The Hebrew Bible in Art* (1944)
1940	Sidney Smith	*Isaiah Chapters XL–LV: Literary Criticism and History* (1944)
1941	Paul E Kahle	*The Cairo Geniza* (1947, second edition 1959)
1942	Wilfred L Knox	*Some Hellenistic Elements in Primitive Christianity* (1944)
1943	William Barron Stevenson	*The Poem of Job: A Literary Study with a New Translation* (1947)
1944	G R Driver	*Semitic Writing, from Pictograph to Alphabet* (1948; revised edition 1954; newly revised edition, edited by S A Hopkins, 1976)
1945	C J Gadd	*Ideas of Divine Rule in the Ancient East* (1948)

[The 1908–1943 & 1945 Lectures were reissued in paperback by Kraus Reprint in 1980.]

1946	G Zuntz	*The Text of the Epistles: A Disquisition upon the Corpus Paulinum* (1953)
1947	S R K Glanville	*The Contribution of Demotic to the Study of Egyptian History* (unpublished)
1948	H H Rowley	*From Joseph to Joshua: Biblical Traditions in the Light of Archaeology* (1950, repr 1951, 1952, 1958, 1964, 1970)
1949	Georges Dossin	*Les Archives de Mari dans ses Rapports avec l'Ancien Testament* (unpublished)
1950	A M Honeyman	*The Phoenicians* (unpublished)
1951	G D Kilpatrick	*The Original Form of the New Testament* (unpublished)
1953	A Dupont-Sommer	*Les Araméens* (unpublished)
1955	M E L Mallowan	*Assyria and the Old Testament* (unpublished)
1957	H-C Puech	*Une collection de Paroles de Jésus récemment découverte: L'Évangile selon Thomas* (unpublished)
1959	Roland de Vaux	*L'Archéologie et les Manuscrits de la Mer Morte* (1961)
		Archaeology and the Dead Sea Scrolls (1973, repr 1977)
1961	A F L Beeston	*Social Organisation of Pre-Islamic South Arabia* (unpublished)
1963	Kathleen M Kenyon	*Amorites and Canaanites* (1966)

1965	Harald Ingholt	*Mari, Ugarit, Hamath: Archaeological Contributions from Ancient Syria to the Old Testament* (unpublished)
1967	Edward Ullendorff	*Ethiopia and the Bible* (1968, repr 1983; pbk edition 1988, repr 1989, 1992, 1997, 2006)
1970	Yigael Yadin	*Hazor* (1972)
1972	Charles Coüasnon	*The Church of the Holy Sepulchre in Jerusalem* (1974)
1974	André Parrot	*Mari et l'Ancien Testament* (unpublished)
1976	O R Gurney	*Some Aspects of Hittite Religion* (1977)
1977	Colin H Roberts	*Manuscript, Society and Belief in Early Christian Egypt* (1979)
1983	D J Wiseman	*Nebuchadrezzar and Babylon* (1985, repr 1987; pbk edition 1991, repr 1995, 2004)
1984	Abraham Malamat	*Mari and the Early Israelite Experience* (1989; pbk edition 1992)

[The published Lectures of 1944, 1946–1963, 1970–1977, 1983 and 1984 are now available from Oxford University Press 'manufactured on demand']

1986	James Barr	*The Variable Spellings of the Hebrew Bible* (1989)
1989	S P Brock	*The Bible in the Syriac Churches* (text awaited)
1992	Henry Chadwick	*Ancient Interpretation of Sacred Books* (web publication 2009)
1995	Michael A Knibb	*Translating the Bible: The Ethiopic Version of the Old Testament* (1999)
1998	Othmar Keel	*Symbol Systems of Ancient Palestine, in the Light of Scarabs and Similar Seal-amulets* (text awaited)
2001	P R S Moorey	*Idols of the People: Miniatures Images of Clay in the Ancient Near East* (2003)
2004	Lawrence Stager	*Ashkelon, Seaport of the Canaanites and the Philistines* (text awaited)
2007	Dennis Pardee	*Ugaritic and the Beginnings of the West-Semitic Literary Tradition* (in press)

CHAPTER 3

ARCHAEOLOGY AND THE BIBLE: A BROKEN LINK?

Terminology

WE HAVE SEEN IN THE previous chapter a little of the range of knowledge that has been brought to public notice by the Schweich Lectures. This third chapter, while not losing sight of the Schweich Lectures and their influence, will explore some more general issues that are raised particularly by the study of archaeology in connection with the Bible. Rather than examining the full extent of such issues (which has been well done by others many times before),[1] my first intention is to examine the changing perceptions over the past century of what (if anything) archaeology can contribute to biblical study. Then it will be possible to ask whether this part of 'the Schweich project' still has any value, and if so how it may most fruitfully be taken forward.

If we are to have a clear and fruitful discussion of the issues raised by the title of the chapter, it is essential to begin by looking more closely at its wording—and that applies as much to its first half as the second. Even the apparently empty word 'and' conceals a multitude of questions. But to begin with 'archaeology', this is a word which has been used in a number of senses. The underlying Greek word was used quite generally for 'the study of ancient times, or antiquity', as for example by the first-century Jewish historian Flavius Josephus for the work more commonly known as his *Jewish Antiquities*, which described the history of the Jews from creation to his own times. In the past two hundred years or so 'archaeology' has come to be used of the discovery of remains of the past history of humanity by

---

1 E.g. recently in J. R. Bartlett (ed.), *Archaeology and Biblical Interpretation* (London, Routledge, 1997).

exploration or excavation. But even now there are variations in its meaning. Sometimes, and especially in popular discussion about relationships with the Bible, it comes to be almost equivalent to the discoveries themselves, for which 'archaeological evidence' would be a more precise term, or to the conclusions based on them. It is in this sense that statements are sometimes made about 'archaeology proving' or 'disproving' the Bible. But to its practitioners, the archaeologists themselves, 'archaeology' would generally mean the academic discipline which finds, studies and interprets what we might broadly describe as 'the material evidence of the human past'. Like other academic disciplines, it has had its own history, with changes in its methods and aims, and competing claims about such matters which have become particularly complex in recent decades. This 'history of archaeology as a discipline' is of considerable importance for under- standing some aspects of our subject and I shall return to it later. Before we leave the term 'archaeology', we should note a further distinction which applies to both the popular and the academic uses of it. In a narrower sense, which is probably more common among specialists, 'archaeology' refers to the discovery and study of non-written material from the past, the ruins, debris and artefacts left by our human ancestors. This limitation to non- written material is of course entirely appropriate and indeed unavoidable in the study of prehistory and of non-literate cultures of more recent times. But a wider use of the term would see it as also applying to the discovery and study of ancient *texts* found in excavations, as they have been, for example, in the case of civilisations of the ancient Near East such as Egypt and Babylonia. Whatever the merits or otherwise of including such study under the heading of archaeology—and there are debates about this too— it has certainly played a very significant part in discussions, both popular and academic, about relations between the Bible and its ancient environment and it would be a serious mistake for us to leave it out of account here, not least because a number of series of Schweich lectures, perhaps even the majority, have dealt precisely with this kind of evidence.

'And the Bible' of course adds further complications, which arise espe- cially from the fact that the Bible is both a religious book, sacred and a source of spiritual truth to both Jews and Christians, and (as has increasingly been realised in modern times) a collection of ancient books, or more precisely two collections of books if we have the Christian Bible in mind, which have become the object of critical and historical study as well as religious devotion. It is possible to distinguish, though not always to separate, different approaches to the issues corresponding to these two characteristics of the Bible. There is the popular religious interest which often, though not always, has looked to archaeological evidence for confirmation of the factual historicity of the biblical narrative, sometimes linked to beliefs about its divine origin and often as a bulwark against what are seen as modern challenges to faith from the natural sciences and even from scholarly study of the Bible itself. And there is this scholarly, academic approach to the Bible itself, whose proper and pure aim is the investigation of the real character and original meaning of the biblical text, which naturally leads it too (or so one would suppose) to an intense interest in what could be discovered about its ancient environment, but with no preconceptions about what the implications of such discoveries might be for biblical studies. So one can see how the 'and' in 'Archaeology and the Bible' might conceal quite different attitudes and expectations in these two clienteles. In the real, as opposed to the ideal, world things have been and continue to be more complicated, because of the overlap between these clienteles. Not surprisingly, many biblical scholars are also religious people and some of them have shared, and nourished, the more popular expectations of what archaeology might have to contribute to beliefs about the Bible. Indeed such popular expectations have played an important part in the past in arousing support, and funding, for archaeological work in the Holy Land, and to some extent they continue to do so.

This leads conveniently to the second part of my title: 'A Broken Link?' The phrase 'broken link' implies, and is meant to imply, an earlier situation in which archaeology and the Bible were seen as integrally related to one another as well as, perhaps, a present-day situation in which this might no longer be the case. In the remainder of this chapter, therefore, I shall address a number of questions about the relations between archaeology and the Bible, past and present. First, looking backwards, what was the nature of the link or links that formerly existed between archaeology and the study of the Bible? Second, what factors challenged and still do challenge such a linkage? Third, how should one assess the present situation? Has the link been broken, and if so does it matter? And fourthly, if it has been broken and it does matter, how might the broken link be repaired? Given the purpose of this volume, I shall use examples from past series of Schweich Lectures as far as possible to examine these issues, and I also propose to focus more on the situation in Britain and Europe than is usually done, so as to complement the extensive and often trenchant literature on the subject that derives from the United States. But I shall not leave the latter entirely out of account, especially in its more recent aspects. I should add that the answers to my four questions will become progressively shorter![2]

The Earlier Linkage between Archaeology and the Study of the Bible

As a former Editor of the *Palestine Exploration Quarterly*, if for no other reason, I must begin with the Palestine Exploration Fund (PEF). Its origins illustrate very well how strong religious support for archaeological work and an initial focus on matters of religious interest could be combined with the determination to uphold high scientific standards which has been characteristic of the British contribution to research in the Holy Land.[3] Founded in 1865, in the immediate aftermath of the controversies sparked off by the publication of *Essays and Reviews* and Darwin's *Origin of Species*, the PEF certainly enjoyed support from dignitaries of the Church of England but also from much wider circles. With only one exception (the American F. J. Bliss) its surveyors and excavators were not biblical scholars. In the early days they were mainly army officers from the Royal Engineers, later they were archaeologists such as Flinders Petrie who were drawn in from other areas of work. Funding came initially from the subscriptions of the members, whose very numbers ensured that policy was not dominated by the interests of any specific group, but followed the principles laid down at the beginning. The sites chosen for excavation included the religious centre of Jerusalem (three times in the first sixty-five years: 1867–70, 1894–7 and 1923–8) but also a series of sites in the south-west of the country such as Tell el-Hesi, Tell el-Jazari and Ain Shems, which were not central to any

---

2 For an excellent, and broader, coverage of the subject up to 1990 I cannot do better than refer to the late Roger Moorey's *A Century of Biblical Archaeology* (Cambridge, Lutterworth, 1991). I have been repeatedly conscious, in my preparation, of following paths which he had already trodden.

3 See more fully, in addition to Moorey's *Century*, my essays on 'British Archaeologists', in Drinkard et al. (eds), *Benchmarks in Time and Culture*, pp. 37–62, and 'The Contribution of the Palestine Exploration Fund to Research on the Holy Land', in U. Hübner (ed.), *Palaestina exploranda. Studien zur Erforschung Palästinas im 19. und 20. Jahrhundert anlässlich des 125jährigen Bestehens des Deutschen Vereins zur Erforschung Palästinas*, Abhandlungen des Deutschen Palästina-Vereins 34 (Wiesbaden, Harrassowitz, 2006), pp. 53–64.

particular biblical issue.[4] The PEF's publications, including the *Quarterly Statement* (*PEFQS*), as it was then known, included biblical material but were by no means dominated by it.

There was of course in the late nineteenth century a good deal of more popular writing, by authors such as H. B. Tristram and George Adam Smith, which sought to correlate the new discoveries with the Bible. But the best of it at least was not so much apologetic as instructive.[5] However, with the increasing prominence on the one hand of the so-called 'Higher Criticism' of the Bible in Britain from about 1880 and the growing quantity of translated texts from ancient Egypt and Babylonia on the other, both a problem and a possible solution from the side of archaeology entered the public debate. A leading part in this debate seems to have been played by Assyriologists such as George Smith and especially A. H. Sayce (1845–1933).[6] Sayce was an Anglican clergyman, who was among the pioneers of Assyriology and especially Hittite studies in Britain. He was successively deputy Professor of Comparative Philology (1876–90) and Professor of Assyriology (1891–1915) at Oxford, and he was the President of the Society for Biblical Archaeology from 1898 until its demise in 1919.[7] If Gladstone, with whom the decision lay, had been a prophet, Sayce would have succeeded E. B. Pusey as Regius Professor of Hebrew at Oxford in 1882, but he did not then seem to measure up to the Prime Minister's requirement for a safe, conservative scholar, and the appointment went to S. R. Driver, a choice which in the long run cannot be regretted.[8] Throughout a scholarly

---

4 It does, however, appear that the choice of Tell el-Hesi in 1890 was influenced by the biblical interests of A. H. Sayce (see below), as has recently been shown by R. S. Hallote, *Bible, Map and Spade: The American Palestine Exploration Society, Frederick Jones Bliss, and the Forgotten Story of Early American Biblical Archaeology* (New Jersey, Gorgias Press, 2006), pp. 100–1.

5 Fuller study of the popular literature of this period is needed.

6 See further Moorey, *Century*, pp. 11–12, 40–4. One might have thought that the foundation of the Society for Biblical Archaeology in 1872 (in which George Smith had a part) was connected with this. But initially at least its publications contained only passing references to directly biblical topics and the emphasis fell on the publication and discussion of newly discovered texts of the most varied periods from the ancient Near East. The *Transactions* of the Society were published from 1872 to 1893 and its *Proceedings* from 1878 to 1918, when they were significantly 'absorbed' into the *Journal of the Royal Asiatic Society*.

7 See Moorey, *Century*, p. 41; more fully *Oxford Dictionary of National Biography* 49, 158–60.

8 On this episode see J. A. Emerton, 'Samuel Rolles Driver', in *A Century of British Orientalists 1902–2001*, ed. C. E. Bosworth (Oxford, OUP for the British Academy,

career of over fifty years Sayce published prolifically on ancient Near Eastern languages, texts, religion and history. His first works devoted specifically to their value for the confirmation of biblical history appeared in the mid-1880s,[9] but it was especially from about a decade later that he produced a series of larger and smaller works with a decisive, and incisive, apologetic tendency. His *The 'Higher Criticism' and the Verdict of the Monuments* first appeared in 1894[10] and went through eight editions, the final one published in 1915. A more popular version of this, *Monument Facts and Higher Critical Fancies*, was issued in 1902,[11] with a fifth and final edition in 1927. It may have been the publication in 1891 of Driver's *Introduction to the Literature of the Old Testament*,[12] which gave respectable commendation to at least the more moderate claims of German criticism, that spurred Sayce into this torrent of replies. His focus then was above all on the antiquity and historical reliability, and indeed the Mosaic authorship, of the Pentateuch, which he held to be established by discoveries such as the Amarna letters and, eventually, the Code of Hammurabi. The correlation of the names of the eastern kings in Genesis 14 with cuneiform sources was also a recurring interest of his (down at least to the final issue of the *Proceedings of the Society of Biblical Archaeology* in 1918). Sayce's writings were undoubtedly seen, to judge from their popularity, in many quarters as a welcome riposte to biblical criticism (which was still widely perceived as criticism of the Bible). In Britain it was above all S. R. Driver who took it upon himself to answer him (Plate 9).[13]

2001), pp. 122–38 (esp. 124–5). If account is taken of the publications of the two scholars up to 1882, it is easier to see why Gladstone (or his advisors) judged them as he did. Driver, in particular, had published nothing by then to suggest that he was anything other than an outstanding Hebrew scholar with a special interest in Jewish interpretation of the Old Testament.

 9 *Fresh Light from the Ancient Monuments. A Sketch of the Most Striking Confirmations of the Bible, from Recent Discoveries in Egypt, Palestine, Assyria, Babylonia, Asia Minor* (London, Religious Tract Society, 1884); *The Witness of Ancient Monuments to the Old Testament Scriptures* (London, Religious Tract Society, 1885).

10 (London, SPCK; New York, E. and J. B. Young, 1894).

11 (London, Religious Tract Society, 1902).

12 (Edinburgh, T. and T. Clark, 1891)

13 See Moorey, *Century*, pp. 40–1, for a similar response by Francis Brown (later one of the editors, with Driver and C. A. Briggs, of the Oxford Hebrew Dictionary) to such claims in the United States, where they seem to have had a longer history (see ibid., p. 3; and now Hallote, *Bible, Map and Spade* [n. 4]).

Nine years before the delivery of his Schweich Lectures, in 1899, Driver had already contributed a long essay to a volume edited by D. G. Hogarth, then the Director of the British School at Athens.[14] This essay was concerned entirely with the evidence of texts brought to light by archaeologists: such other results of excavations as there were at this time were ignored. This was at least in part due to the agenda which Sayce had set in his publications, and Driver's detailed discussion here follows the order of the biblical books: the Pentateuch, sub-divided into Genesis 1–11, Genesis 12–50, Exodus and 'Evidence of Canaan', followed by 'The Kings and After', which concludes with an impressive selection of 'Aramaic and Phoenician texts'.[15] As he proceeded, he assessed the significance of each 'parallel', noting how the new evidence sometimes raised difficulties for the precise historical reliability of the biblical narrative as well as confirming other details. His considered conclusion (pp. 143–52) has often been cited as a remarkably clear and fitting assessment of the significance of non-biblical evidence for the understanding of the Old Testament, or to be more precise for the resolving of historical and critical issues. The principles laid down there mainly relate to what external evidence has and has not *proved*, and according to Driver it had not proved very much, only things that no one had ever doubted.[16]

The title of the published form of Driver's Schweich Lectures of 1908 seems to have been deliberately chosen to shift discussion away from such claims: *Modern Research as Illustrating the Bible*.[17] As he put it in the first lecture: 'The really important and valuable archaeological discoveries are not those which merely corroborate isolated biblical statements, the correctness of which has never been challenged; but those which rectify or

---

14 'Hebrew Authority', in D. G. Hogarth (ed.), *Authority and Archaeology: Sacred and Profane* (London, John Murray, 1899), pp. 1–152.

15 Even earlier, in 1888, Driver had discussed the inscriptions of the Assyrian kings at length in his *Isaiah, His Life and Times, and the Writings which Bear His Name* (London, Nisbet, 1888, repr. 1893).

16 *Authority*, p. 150: cf. *Modern Research as Illustrating the Bible*, The Schweich Lectures 1908 (London, OUP for the British Academy, 1909), p. 16; also *Introduction* (9th edn, 1913), pp. XVIII–XXI.

17 The lectures themselves had a slightly different title 'The Results of Archaeological Research as Bearing on the Study of the Old Testament' (*Proceedings of the British Academy* 3 [1907–8], p. 11), which had in fact been proposed to Driver by the Academy (minutes of Council 4.7.1907). An appreciative review of the volume by D. D. Luckenbill appeared in *Biblical World* 34/3 (1909), 211–13.

supplement the biblical statements, and especially those which enable us to form a picture of the history and civilisation of the East as a whole and of the place taken by Israel in it, and of the nature of the influence which, as we now see, it exerted upon Israel' (p. 16). In his introduction, revealingly, Driver set his subject in the context of the great expansion of knowledge and research in general during the nineteenth century, both in the sciences and in the study of 'ancient civilisation', not least in the Near East. He was clearly fascinated by the latter for its own sake, and he gives a lengthy account of it (pp. 1–16) before turning to its specific relevance to the Bible. He begins once again with textual evidence from Babylonia and Egypt, but more briefly than in his earlier essay, and his selection and arrangement of examples is now dictated by his own view of what is important rather than the requirements of controversy: the annals of Assyrian kings (at length), the Mesha stele from Moab, Babylonian accounts of the Creation and Flood, inscriptions from Ephesus, texts of Cyrus, evidence of early Babylonian history including the newly discovered laws of Hammurabi, the even more recent finds of Aramaic papyrus letters from Elephantine in Upper Egypt, and the excavations at Ashur and Boghaz-köy, ancient capitals of the Assyrians and the Hittites respectively. 'Illustration' of the Bible is in fact too weak a description for the implications which these texts have for biblical study: they often require a new understanding of biblical passages, and in some cases strongly suggest that the accounts are based on foreign materials, though as Driver repeatedly says, these are 'transformed by the magic touch of Israel's religion, and infused by it with a new spirit' (p. 23).[18]

The second and third lectures were jointly entitled 'Canaan, as known through inscriptions and excavation'. What Driver says about inscriptions (chiefly the Amarna letters and some other texts from Egypt) is used with a historian's insight to shed light on 'the condition of Canaan before the Hebrew occupation', a subject on which the Old Testament was largely silent, and already here the conclusion is drawn that though they were 'divided religiously, the Hebrews and the Canaanites were in language and civilisation closely allied' (p. 37), which sounds very up-to-date in 2010! But the really new and ground-breaking contribution of these lectures was their much fuller account of the material culture of Canaan as it had been exhibited by the results of excavations, mainly those at Tell el-Jazari,

---

18 Driver no doubt had the 'Babel–Bibel' controversy in mind here: he alludes more fully to the issue on p. 90 n.1.

identified with Gezer, which were conducted by R. A. S. Macalister for the PEF from 1902 to 1909, but also those at Tell el-Hesi (1890–3) and Taanach (1902–4).[19] Driver's achievement was all the greater in that the excavations at Gezer had not been completed and so the comprehensive excavation reports had not yet appeared.[20] He therefore relied and drew upon the successive annual reports in the *PEFQS*, with the attendant need to organise this diverse material into his own synthesis of the results (pp. 46–80). This synthesis reflects a breadth of interest which might seem more natural for an archaeologist than the biblical scholar that Driver was (see also his summary on pp. 86–88), and at times he takes Macalister to task for questionable interpretations of his finds, as not a few others have done since! But he does not forget his brief here any more than in discussing the textual evidence earlier, and there is an understandable emphasis on data illustrating religious beliefs and practices, particularly of the Canaanites (pp. 56–73),[21] as well as on inscribed material (pp. 74–80, 82–3). Moreover, in expressing his hope for further useful discoveries, he mentions especially 'some native Canaanite or Hebrew inscriptions' and 'further monuments of Canaanite or Israelite practices' (p. 91).

In summing up Driver again makes a point which will have provided his audience with a general perspective on the impact of the new discoveries, namely that while the evidence of material culture indicated a high degree of continuity between Canaanites and Israelites (as, he argues, 'careful study of the Old Testament itself leads us to expect'), from a religious point of view 'there was a great gulf fixed, which, if possible, has been widened rather than narrowed by the new knowledge that has come to us' (p. 90— cf. pp. 84, 87). Thus for him as well as for Sayce archaeology and biblical study are complementary, rather than in tension. The difference is that Driver

---

19 Only passing reference is made to other early excavations.

20 They were published as R. A. S. Macalister, *The Excavation of Gezer I–III* (London, John Murray for the PEF, 1912). Driver's was not quite the first attempt to survey excavation results from a number of sites: see F. J. Bliss, *The Development of Palestine Exploration* (London, Hodder and Stoughton, 1906), which included excavations as well as travels and surveys, and H. Vincent, *Canaan d'après l'exploration récente* (Paris, Gabalda, 1907), both of which were known to Driver, as were works of Kittel (1908: p. 66) and Sellin (1905: p. 86 n. 1).

21 So at least it was thought at the time. But while the main 'high place' at Gezer with its standing stones continues to be recognised as such, the evidence of the female figurines has sometimes been understood differently in more recent times—see below on Roger Moorey's Schweich Lectures.

sees archaeology contributing to biblical study in a variety of ways: it 'illustrates, supplements, confirms, or corrects, statements or representations contained in the Bible' and helps 'to distinguish narratives in the Bible which are contemporary with the events recorded from those which are of later date' (p. 89). This contrasts sharply with Sayce's one-sided (and often illusory) emphasis on confirmation alone.

As we have seen already, not all the subsequent Schweich Lectures dealt with archaeology (in its narrower senses) and the Bible, but with other topics permitted by the Trust Deed. Still a good number did discuss aspects of the issues before us here and it is time now to give a brief overview of the topics considered in them and the approaches adopted. Initially we will consider only the period from 1909 to 1970: the latter date marks a point at which major changes in the aims and methods of archaeology generally were beginning to have an impact on its practice in the Near East. I want in this survey to begin by looking at the focus or approach of the lecturers to their task, in other words the kind of topics which they spoke about, and then I shall go on to consider the kinds of contribution (if any) which they claimed that archaeology could make to biblical studies. It is worth prefacing these remarks by noting that very few of the archaeological series have dealt with relations with the New Testament—only 1926 in part, 1930, 1937, 1957 and (though not explicitly) 1959, nothing since. This could be put down to a lack of interest in archaeology by New Testament scholars at one time, though there is no lack of material that can be brought to bear on, for example, the Acts of the Apostles and the Pauline Corpus. Sir William Ramsay (1851–1939) was a notable example of a scholar of an earlier generation who used archaeology and especially epigraphy to elucidate the New Testament, and it is remarkable that he was never invited to give the Schweich Lectures, despite being one of the founding Fellows of the British Academy. In more recent times the archaeological context of the New Testament has received much more attention,[22] and it is all the more surprising that this subject has been neglected for so long in the Schweich Lectures.

---

22 Examples would be E. A. Judge and W. A. Meeks, who again worked mainly with inscriptions, the architectural study of P. Richardson, *Building Jewish in the Roman East* (Waco, Baylor University Press, 2004), and J. H. Charlesworth (ed.), *Jesus and Archaeology* (Grand Rapids, Eerdmans, 2006). I am grateful to the late Professor Graham Stanton for some helpful comments on this issue.

We may first note that the most common approach taken in the Schweich Lectures was from outside to in, rather than from inside to out—in other words relatively few lecturers started with a biblical topic or problem and sought for 'external evidence' to clarify or solve it. Examples of the latter are limited to Kennett in 1909, Smith in 1940 (both concerned with the book of Isaiah), Burney in 1917 and Rowley in 1948 (with reference to the history of Israel's early period, 'From Joseph to Joshua', to use Rowley's title). One might perhaps add Cook in 1925 on 'The Religion of Ancient Palestine', though I am inclined to put that into another group of lectures which examined the archaeological 'background' to the Bible in an illustrative rather than an argumentative way, the others being Robinson et al. in 1926, Sukenik in 1930, Crowfoot in 1937 (both of these actually dealt with post-biblical evidence) and G. R. Driver in 1944.

The remaining series have taken their starting-point clearly from outside the Bible, in ways which are not always easy to separate but which do broadly correspond to some general published syntheses of archaeological evidence from the ancient Near East (all initiated by the Society for Old Testament Study (SOTS)), as I shall point out in passing. No less than ten series up to 1970 dealt with evidence for various non-Israelite *peoples*: the Philistines (1911), the Hittites (mainly the Neo-Hittites in south-eastern Turkey and Syria: 1918, 1924), the Iranians (1934), the (late) Egyptians (1947), the Phoenicians (1950), the Aramaeans (1953), the Assyrians (1955), the ancient South Arabians (1961) and the Amorites and Canaanites (1963).[23] Most of the more recent series in this group were unfortunately not published. The approach adopted is close to that of the essays in the volume *Peoples of Old Testament Times*, edited by D. J. Wiseman.[24] A second group of the archaeological lectures dealt with particular kinds of non-biblical *texts* and their importance for biblical studies: Mesopotamian legal texts (1912), the Elephantine papyri (1914), Near Eastern, especially Sumerian, myths (1916), Egyptian literature (1929), Babylonian calendrical texts (1933), ritual texts from Babylonia and Ugarit (1935), Mesopotamian texts about gods and kings (1945) and the Coptic Gospel of Thomas (1957), the last unpublished. Here there is a close correspondence to the SOTS volume *Documents from Old Testament Times*, edited by D. Winton Thomas,[25] as

23 This approach was also taken by a non-archaeological series on the Samaritans (1923).
24 (Oxford, Clarendon Press, 1973).
25 (London, Thomas Nelson, 1958).

well as to some more comprehensive collections of texts in translation published elsewhere, Thirdly, some lecturers spoke about particular sites. In several cases the main focus was on the texts discovered there, so that there is an overlap with the previous category. Much of S. R. Driver's material had come form one site, Gezer, but no further lectures of this kind were given until Schaeffer's on Ugarit in 1936. Further examples dealt with the Cairo Geniza (1941), Mari (1949), Mari, Ugarit and Hamath (1965) and Hazor (1970). This approach corresponds to the layout of *Archaeology and Old Testament Study*, again edited by D. Winton Thomas.[26]

Such an analysis already highlights two features which are characteristic of archaeological studies generally in the first two-thirds of the twentieth century, and severely challenged in the decades that followed. The first is the prominence given to the history and culture of particular peoples, which fitted well into the 'cultural-historical' approach of the time, which has been seen as a product of an increasing 'nationalist' consciousness in Europe as well as an awareness of the diversity of human cultural developments in the past.[27] The second factor is the dominating interest in written texts discovered by archaeologists, as distinct from the evidence of material culture, and the study of these texts in conjunction with the long-known literature of the Bible that had been handed down continuously from antiquity. This corresponded closely to at least an important aspect of classical archaeology. An emphasis on the material culture is much less evident, though interestingly it was prominent in Driver's inaugural series.[28] Later we find it only in Cook (1925), Sukenik (1930), Herzfeld (1934), Crowfoot (1937), de Vaux (1959), Kenyon (1963) and Yadin (1970).

What then did the lecturers suppose that archaeology could contribute to biblical study? The answer sometimes seems to be 'nothing', or very little. The two series on the Hittites (1918, 1924) include very few references to the Bible and the same is true of much of the series on Iran (1934). In a different way one might say the same about the series on synagogues, churches, and the archaeology of Qumran (1930, 1937, 1959), which deal

---

26 (Oxford, Clarendon Press, 1967).

27 See B. Trigger, *A History of Archaeological Thought*, 2nd edn (Cambridge, CUP, 2006), ch. 6, esp. p. 211.

28 There is a hint at the beginning of L. W. King's 1916 lectures that some criticism was already being voiced then about the neglect of material culture in previous lectures: *Legends of Babylon and Egypt in Relation to Hebrew Tradition*, The Schweich Lectures 1916 (London, OUP for the British Academy, 1918), p. v.

with post-biblical developments in Judaism and Christianity. At any rate there is little if any engagement with biblical study in them, even if what was said had (and has) the potential for correlation with biblical issues. This actually has considerable importance, because it shows particularly clearly how discoveries from the ancient world were valued in their own right as subjects of public interest, and not only to serve the purposes of biblical research. In that sense (and it is not true only of these striking examples) the Schweich Lecturers recognised the independence of the study of the ancient Near East from biblical studies already early in the twentieth century, even if this involved some departure from the declared purpose of the Fund.

But in the majority of cases a stronger connection with the Bible is made, though in a variety of ways. It is interesting to observe that most of the approaches taken had been anticipated in Driver's masterly summary at the end of his 1908 lectures (above, p. 44–5), to which Cook in 1925 made specific reference.[29] New discoveries were seen by some as providing the means for solving biblical issues such as the composition of Isaiah (1909) or the chronology of Israel's origins (1917, 1948). More generally they could provide knowledge of the background (Robinson in 1926 spoke specifically of the 'secular' background) against which the religious developments in the Bible took place (1925, 1926, 1944). This applied especially to unprejudiced information about Israel's neighbours, which could correct popular misconceptions based on the Bible: the point is made explicitly by Macalister on the Philistines in 1911. It could even apply to misconceptions about ancient Judaism itself, as van Hoonacker argued from the 'unortho-dox' practice of the Elephantine community in his 1914 lectures (though he saw Samaritan influence as largely responsible for deviations from the 'norm').

Another recurring strand in the lectures was a consideration of how far parts of the Old Testament were dependent upon writings and practices of the Babylonians and Canaanites in particular. This issue was already raised by Johns in 1912, specifically in relation to the laws of Hammurabi and the Book of the Covenant in Exodus. He shows considerable awareness of different views about the critical issues involved in such comparisons as well as in biblical scholarship itself. At one point he seems to anticipate later debates by setting out in a general way the alternatives of separate

---

29 *The Religion of Ancient Palestine in the Light of Archaeology*, The Schweich Lectures 1925 (London, OUP for the British Academy, 1930), p. v.

development or the diffusion of ideas from one culture to another.[30] His own tentative conclusion is that both Exodus and the laws of Hammurabi were separately dependent on an earlier Babylonian original. Four years later (in 1916) King addressed similar questions in a comparison of Genesis 1–11 with Mesopotamian literature, concluding that the closest parallel to the overall pattern of creation followed by a flood was in a then recently published Sumerian text[31] but that it was in Semitic, i.e. Babylonian, versions that closer parallels of detail could be found. Again the general issues about the likelihood of such dependence and the most probable periods for borrowing to have taken place receive careful consideration. Cook's lectures of 1925 on 'The Religion of Ancient Palestine in the Light of Archaeology' make a similar point on the basis of material culture—he speaks of the 'single canvas' and the 'single stream', which emphasised both what Israel shared with its neighbours and the possibility of long-term comparisons through time (p. 7). He was probably the biblical scholar of that period who stood closest to the results of excavations: archaeology for him raises 'new questions' and he is more alive than some to the problems of interpreting archaeological evidence.[32]

The issue of dependence came to the fore again in lectures given in the 1930s, partly due to the dramatic discoveries of texts at Ras Shamra/Ugarit from 1929 and their decipherment. In 1933 Langdon showed how a variety of local calendars in Mesopotamia had been replaced by that of Nippur (itself of ultimately Sumerian origin) and that this was adopted by biblical scribes in the Neo-Babylonian period, among other things for fixing the dates of their religious festivals. One such festival, later known as Tesha b'Av, he claimed to be based on a specific Babylonian festival. Two years later, in 1935, S. H. Hooke took such thinking a stage further by suggesting that the whole of early Israelite religion was shaped by 'the influence of the culture pattern dominant in the Near East' in the mid-2nd millennium B.C.[33]

---

30 C. H. W. Johns, *The Relations between the Laws of Babylonia and the Laws of the Hebrew Peoples*, The Schweich Lectures 1912 (London, OUP for the British Academy, 1914), p. 54.

31 For which see now W. G. Lambert and A. R. Millard, *Atrahasis: The Babylonian Story of the Flood* (Oxford, Clarendon Press, 1969), p. 14.

32 His long period as Editor of the *PEFQS* (1902–32) undoubtedly contributed to his familiarity with the subject.

33 S. H. Hooke, *The Origins of Early Semitic Ritual*, The Schweich Lectures 1935 (London, OUP for the British Academy, 1938), p. ix.

Comparisons with non-biblical material were 'supplementing, and to some extent superseding' the results of biblical criticism in a way that, he argued, was 'only now beginning to be recognised'. Mesopotamia had influenced Canaan and Canaan had influenced Israel, and awareness of this made it possible to detect behind the biblical text substantial remnants of myth and ritual which were little different from their Canaanite equivalents. The novelty of Hooke's proposals lay not so much in their general character, which had been anticipated by scholars such as Gunkel and Mowinckel, as in the extent to which he was prepared to press them, as can be seen also in his other writings on the subject. But the new texts could also be understood as supporting the reliability of the Bible, as well as undermining its originality. In the following year, 1936, the lectures were given by C. F. A. Schaeffer on the excavations at Ugarit which he himself had directed. They were more cautious and factual than Hooke's had been and when it came to implications for biblical study his conclusions were much more conservative. He held that the library of written texts from Ugarit (as others had earlier claimed about the Amarna letters) showed that Wellhausen's late dating of Genesis and its sources was unfounded. 'One can no longer doubt the antiquity of the patriarchal narratives. . .', which in his view dealt with 'real events'.[34] He also gave a new twist to observations about similarities between the Canaanites and Israelites: the Ugaritic texts showed a 'high moral tone' and a piety which 'is equal to that of Abraham'. Only in the time of Moses did Israel become distinct, and the biblical writers' portrayal of the Canaanites was designed to conceal their indebtedness to them.[35]

The lectures of Schaeffer mark the beginning of a lengthy period in which a somewhat higher regard for the biblical text, in relation to archaeology (and biblical criticism), is discernible in the Schweich Lectures.[36]

---

34 *The Cuneiform Texts of Ras Shamra-Ugarit*, The Schweich Lectures 1936 (London, OUP for the British Academy, 1939), p. 58.

35 Ibid., p. 59. Some more recent specialists in Ugaritic have argued along similar lines, e.g. F. M. Cross, J. C. de Moor, M. S. Smith.

36 So at least it appears from the published lectures. Whether, for example, Puech's 1957 series on the Gospel of Thomas would fit into such a picture must remain uncertain. A later publication of Puech's lectures in Paris suggests that he was particularly interested in the interpretation of the Gospel and its (Gnostic) theology in their own right: H.-C. Puech, *En quête de la Gnose. II Sur l'évangile selon Thomas. Esquisse d'une interpretation systématique*, Bibliothèque des sciences humaines (Paris, Gallimard, 1978). I am indebted to Dr Simon Gathercole for this information.

Before turning to this, however, we should look back a few years to a series of lectures which in two ways took a rather different tack from those just summarised. These were those of Peet in 1929. Their focus was on Egypt rather than Babylonia and Canaan, and Peet was more interested in a general comparison than in establishing dependence of the Bible on non-biblical texts. To this end he presented a comprehensive survey of Egyptian literature, illustrated by many translations of texts, divided into categories of epic or myth, short story, lyric (including love poetry) and, Egypt's 'highest literary distinction', wisdom. He concluded that comparison with the Old Testament highlighted its exclusively religious focus, which contrasted with the much wider range of the Egyptian texts and their nature as 'literature for literature's sake'.

The change to which I alluded a moment ago corresponds, though in a lesser degree, to the rise of 'Biblical Archaeology' in the United States and elsewhere, under the leadership especially of W. F. Albright and his pupil G. E. Wright. Although this expression could (as it probably did in the early years of the Schweich Lectures: see above) simply mean archaeological evidence from the historical context of the Bible, it came in the United States and elsewhere to imply an approach in which the Bible and a perceived need to defend its historical accuracy set the agenda (see the beginning of this chapter). Sidney Smith's lectures on Isaiah 40–55 (1940), while fully accepting the critical arguments for a Neo-Babylonian date for these chapters, begin with a vigorous challenge to some recent scholarly work on them. But his main argument is that this section of the Bible is a valuable historical source, alongside Babylonian documents, for understanding the politics and military campaigns which led to the conquest of Babylon by Cyrus of Persia. Moreover, the prophet's support for Cyrus was a direct cause of Cyrus's favourable attitude to the Jews thereafter. One might perhaps see Kahle's and G. R. Driver's lectures (1941 and 1944) on the biblical text and its written form as part of this trend, with their focus on the Bible in its external form. Rowley's 1948 series on early Israelite history certainly engaged with a central scholarly issue of the day and, while in outline his conclusions followed closely those of Burney in 1917, he could make much more use of the results of excavations and surveys in his argument, particularly those carried out by the Americans in the 1920s and 1930s. His treatment of the biblical sources did (again like Burney's) allow for some merging and reshaping of traditions that had originally referred to separate stages in Israel's origins, but in general it assumed that there was a much closer correspondence between the texts and actual history than German scholars like A. Alt and M. Noth had recently been suggesting.[37]

The same tendency appears in two later series of Schweich Lectures which were given by archaeologists who had led major excavations in Palestine itself in the 1950s, Kathleen Kenyon and Yigael Yadin, undoubtedly the two leading figures in the field then outside America. Kenyon in 1963 took a fresh approach to the Canaanite civilisation encountered and adopted by the 'infiltrating' Israelites (p. 77) by asking where it had itself come from. Her answer was that it too had originated in the infiltration of outsiders, in fact in two waves of newcomers from respectively inland and coastal Syria. Their appearance could be seen archaeologically in two successive cultural phases which were very evident in her own excavations at Jericho, but also elsewhere, the so-called 'Intermediate Early Bronze-Middle Bronze' period (known by others as EB IV or MB I or a combination of the two) and the Middle Bronze Age proper (MB II to others). Two aspects of her conclusions deserve note here. First, in the sphere of purely archaeological interpretation her explanation of these cultural changes by the migration of peoples from further north was a classic example of the 'diffusionist' thinking which was characteristic of cultural-historical archaeology, and it is one which has continued to be a focus of debate.[38] But secondly, Kenyon made a correlation between these artefactual assemblages and the 'peoples' which they represent and the biblical names 'Amorites' and 'Canaanites'. These names not only gave her the title for her lectures but the areas where they are attested in the Bible were held by her to correspond to what she called 'two archaeological provinces', basically the central highlands and Transjordan on the one hand and the coastal plain and other

37 See Noth's polite but devastating review of *From Joseph to Joshua* in *VT* 1 (1951), 74–80; Albright's brief assessment in *Bulletin of the American Schools of Oriental Research* 121 (1951), 25 was by contrast much more appreciative.

38 For criticism of Kenyon's approach see J. N. Tubb, 'The MBIIA Period in Palestine: its Relationship with Syria and its Origin', *Levant* 15 (1983), 49–62; Moorey, *Century*, p. 123; on the other hand '(t)his antidiffusionist way of thinking, perhaps inspired by C. Renfrew's approach to developments in European archaeology' is itself criticised by A. Mazar, *Archaeology of the Land of the Bible 10,000–586 B.C.E.* (New York, Doubleday, 1990), pp. 169–71, 188–9 (the quoted phrases come from p. 173 n. 24). A recent biography of Kenyon notes her high regard for the Bible: see M. C. Davis, *Dame Kathleen Kenyon: Digging Up the Holy Land* (Walnut Creek, Left Coast Press, 2008), pp. 20, 63, though p. 117 shows that she could be more detached.

low-lying areas on the other. Again the Bible is being seen as a reliable historical source which can even help with problems of archaeological interpretation.

This is much more extensively the case in Yadin's 1970 lectures on his excavations at Hazor. Yadin too was by no means only interested in findings which he could correlate with the Bible, but already in his summary of the main evidence from Hazor for the Canaanite period (pp. 106–7) it is prominent that 'Its description in the Bible as the "head of all those kingdoms" [a phrase from Joshua 11.10] is evidently historically correct'. Historical (he means textual) evidence generally is highly regarded by Yadin: he summarises it before he gives a basic description of the site (pp. 1–12) and in his overall conclusion he states that 'Historical data are absolute, while the archaeological material. . .is not always as definitive as we might have wished' (p. 198). Despite some cautionary remarks which are often overlooked—he here regards the correlation between the destruction of Canaanite Hazor and Joshua 11 as only 'probable' (ibid.) and he allows that the typical Iron I pottery in Palestine is not 'exclusively Israelite in the *ethnical* sense' (p. 131 n. 3)—Yadin's whole account of the Iron Age is prominently related to biblical accounts of the history of Israel in the Judges and Monarchy periods (see the Contents, pp. xii–xiii). The most famous and now controversial example is the identification of Stratum X as 'the Solomonic city' (e.g. pp. 134–5). The Bible interprets archaeology, and archaeology confirms the historicity of the Bible.

But changes which were by then in the air, both in biblical studies and in archaeology, put fresh strains on the generally close link between archaeology and biblical study which had existed hitherto.

Factors which Challenged the Link between Archaeology and the Study of the Bible

It may not be entirely coincidental that the 1960s, which in Western society generally were a time of rapid and unsettling changes, also saw the beginnings of new developments in both archaeology and biblical studies. These developments tended to move interest away from questions about the relationship between the two disciplines and in their more extreme forms have led to doubts about whether such questions can be raised at all, as was well observed by Joachim Schaper in his study of current research on the history of Israel.[39] On the archaeological side changes which began in the study of prehistory brought archaeology firmly into the domain of the social sciences, especially anthropology and geography. In the United States Lewis Binford was the leader of a movement which became known as 'New Archaeology'.[40] Sometimes the more specific term 'processual archaeology' is used, because of the centrality of cultural processes and their explanation in this approach to archaeology. It subordinated the study of particular societies to the quest for generalised explanations of systemic change, which were based on ecological factors rather than on the diffusion of cultural traits and the migration of individual peoples. The development of such explanations required both an intensive use of scientific knowledge and observation and also a training in ethnology, since it was by studying the interaction between living societies, their artefacts and their natural environment that a basis could, it was thought, be established for sound generalised inferences from the archaeological evidence. This model for explanation was drawn from the natural sciences and led to a strong antipathy to historical studies that were focused on particular events and societies. In Britain David Clarke and Colin Renfrew led the way in changes of perspective which were similar but less far-reaching than those just described.[41] These new approaches offered ways of accounting for the human past, and indeed human existence as such, which had all the certainties of science and beside which text-based studies could seem to have a very insecure basis. In consequence, the very idea of a 'Biblical Archaeology' came to appear out-dated and inferior in America, and William Dever, an archaeologist working in the Middle East who was an enthusiastic convert to the new ideas, campaigned for its replacement by 'Syro-Palestinian Archaeology', to emphasise the independence of what he and his colleagues were doing from texts in general and the Bible in particular.[42] It is a measure of the different situation in Britain that the

---

39 'Auf der Suche nach dem alten Israel? Text, Artefakt und "Geschichte Israels" in der alttestamentlichen Wissenschaft vor dem Hintergrund der Methodendiskussion in der Historischen Kulturwissenschaften', *Zeitschrift für die Alttestamentliche Wissenschaft* 118 (2006), 1–21, 181–96, esp. 181–3. For the wider background see Trigger, *History*, pp. 409–13.

40 See Trigger, *History*, pp. 392–410. For the points which follow see pp. 394–5, 399 and 400–1.

41 Trigger, *History*, pp. 430–6.

42 Dever made his case in a succession of writings from *Archaeology and Biblical Studies: Retrospects and Prospects* (Evanston, Seabury-Western Theological Seminary, 1974) to 'The Impact of the "New Archaeology"', in Drinkard et al. (eds), *Benchmarks in Time*

post which Kathleen Kenyon held at the Institute of Archaeology in London from 1948 to 1962 was already then known as 'Lecturer in Palestinian Archaeology'.

The link between archaeology and biblical studies was also put under strain by developments in the biblical field.[43] There were two strands to these developments, one internal to the discipline and one due to wider influences from the humanities in general. On the one hand the scholarly consensus about a number of central issues in Old Testament studies—such as the 'amphictyony' in the Judges period, the antiquity of the Sinai covenant, the dating and even the existence of the traditional sources of the Pentateuch, the centrality of history in biblical theology—was challenged or even over-thrown, with the result that the study of Israelite history gradually became to some a less attractive and less central aspect of the discipline and to others (the so-called 'minimalists') a subject to which the biblical narratives could no longer make a significant contribution.[44] At the same time the potential of the various kinds of approaches to texts fostered in the study of modern literature came to be increasingly recognised by biblical scholars, especially in the United States and Britain, and among them those based on 'reader response' tended to sit very loose to the original historical meaning and context of a text, and so to any interest in its correlation (or lack of it) with archaeological evidence. Not surprisingly archaeologists came to doubt whether there was anything of interest to them in the biblical texts, even

---

and Culture, pp. 337–52. The final 'triumph' of this approach came in 1998, when the popular journal of the American Schools of Oriental Research, founded by Albright in 1938 with the title *The Biblical Archaeologist*, changed its name to *Near Eastern Archaeology*.

43 On these see, e.g., J. Barton, *Reading the Old Testament: Method in Biblical Study*, 2nd edn (London, Darton, Longman and Todd, 1996), esp. chs 6–14; J. Barton (ed.), *The Cambridge Companion to Biblical Interpretation* (Cambridge, CUP, 1998).

44 On the theories of the scholars whom their opponents dubbed 'minimalists', such as P. R. Davies and T. L. Thompson, see J. Barr, *History and Ideology in the Old Testament: Biblical Studies at the End of a Millennium* (Oxford, OUP, 2000), pp. 59–101, and the overview by Finkelstein in I. Finkelstein and A. Mazar, *The Quest for the Historical Israel: Debating Archaeology and the History of Early Israel*, ed. B. B. Schmidt (Atlanta, Society of Biblical Literature, 2007), pp. 12–14, as well as Dever's extended critique in W. G. Dever, *What Did the Biblical Writers Know and When Did They Know It?* (Grand Rapids, Eerdmans, 2001), ch. 2, which points out (pp. 43–4) that Finkelstein's own 'low chronology' has been cited in support of the newer views, although he dissociates himself from them.

when they did not sideline textual evidence altogether.[45] Thus on both sides there have been strong tendencies pulling archaeology and biblical studies away from each other.

An Assessment of the Present Situation

So has the link between archaeology and Biblical studies in fact been broken since these new developments began? As far as the situation in Britain is concerned, the Schweich Lectures given in the 1970s and early 1980s at least suggest not. The topics that were covered maintained familiar approaches from the past: the study of a particular site (Coüasnon 1972 [admittedly a post-biblical one], Parrot 1974, Wiseman 1983, Malamat 1984) or evidence of an ancient people from the biblical world (Gurney 1976). Was this because in Britain a separation between archaeology and biblical studies had not taken place? There were certainly some other signs of a continuing interest in links between the disciplines. For example, around 1980 it was still possible to assemble a group of authors to write books on 'Cities of the Biblical World', though perhaps it is significant that all those who wrote on particular sites were biblical scholars.[46] And a sign of some distancing of archaeology and biblical studies might be seen in the absence of any archaeological topics in the Schweich Lectures between 1984 and 1998. It is true that this was not a permanent change, and in fact all the last four series have been archaeological in the broad sense, as we shall see in a moment. But three of the recent lecturers had to be brought from abroad and the fourth, Roger Moorey, is very sadly no longer with us.

In the world of British Near Eastern archaeology generally there were changes around 1970 but, at least to begin with, they were of a different nature and had different causes from what was happening in America.[47]. At the same time as Kathleen Kenyon was directing her landmark excavations at Jericho and Jerusalem, two younger scholars, Diana Kirkbride

45 E.g. Moorey, *Century*, p. 173; Finkelstein and Mazar, *The Quest for the Historical Israel*, pp. 5–8 (with reference to the earlier periods of biblical history).
46 The exception which 'proves the rule' was Moorey's *Excavation in Palestine* (Guildford, Lutterworth, 1981): at this stage Moorey's treatment of the 'New Archaeology' (p. 18) remained brief and cautious.
47 I am grateful to Mr P. J. Parr and Dr K. Prag for comments after my lecture which drew my attention to these differences.

and Peter Parr, were also undertaking work of their own at two sites in southern Jordan, el-Beidha and Petra, which proved to be of enormous importance for the study of, respectively, the Mesolithic and Pre-Pottery Neolithic B periods and the civilisation of the Nabataeans. Although British archaeologists had worked in Jordan before, the work at these sites helped to broaden archaeological perspectives both chronologically and geo-graphically, and the largely unexcavated ancient remains of Jordan were a most inviting prospect. It was natural that in 1974 the British School of Archaeology in Jerusalem opened an office in Amman and four years later it became an independent institution as the British Institute at Amman for Archaeology and History. It was increasingly from here that British archaeological work in the Levant was carried on, while the Jerusalem School busied itself with architectural surveys in Jerusalem itself and else-where west of the Jordan valley. Initially the new work in Jordan continued to add to knowledge and understanding of the biblical period, as excavations at Tawilan, Buseirah and elsewhere between 1968 and 1982, directed by Mrs C. M. Bennett, for the first time brought the material culture of the kingdom of Edom clearly into view.[48] But the emphasis of British work came gradually to rest more on earlier and later periods, including the study of prehistory.[49] There may at this stage have been more of a connection with the impact of the new methods and approaches mentioned earlier. This can also be seen in the criticisms of Kathleen Kenyon's 'diffusionist' Schweich Lectures by Jonathan Tubb and Roger Moorey.[50] Elsewhere Moorey reflects well the growing awareness and understanding of the new developments among British Near Eastern archaeologists and their qualified reception of

48 For a brief account of this work until 1983 see my 'British Archaeologists' in Drinkard et al. (eds), *Benchmarks in Time and Culture*, pp. 47, 54–9. More up-to-date information can be found on the website of the Council for British Research in the Levant (www.cbrl.org.uk). On Crystal Bennett see K. Prag, 'Crystal-M. Bennett OBE, BA, D.LITT., FSA: A Memoir', *Palestine Exploration Quarterly* 142 (2010), 43–63.

49 The main exceptions to this have been the joint excavation of Tel Jezreel with Tel Aviv University between 1990 and 1996 (see D. Ussishkin, 'Jezreel, Samaria and Megiddo: Royal Cities of Omri and Ahab' in J. A. Emerton (ed.), *Congress Volume Cambridge 1995*, Supplements to Vetus Testamentum 66 (Leiden, Brill, 1997), pp. 351–64) and Jonathan Tubb's excavation (on behalf of the British Museum) of important Late Bronze and Iron Age levels at Tell es-Sa'idiyeh in the Jordan valley since 1985 (for convenient summaries of the results see J. N. Tubb, *Canaanites* [Peoples of the Past: London, British Museum Press, 1998], pp. 82–91, 96–100, 115, 124–7).

50 See above, n. 37.

them.[51] Perhaps another sign of the independence and professionalism of Palestinian archaeology in Britain could be seen in the establishment of a new journal, *Levant*, by the British School of Archaeology in Jerusalem in 1968 as a vehicle for technical archaeological reports which had previously appeared in the more broadly based *Palestine Exploration Quarterly*, whose editors have tended to be biblical scholars. But we must remember that in Britain the subject had long been based in secular environments such as the Institute of Archaeology in London (founded in 1937) and various University departments of archaeology, so there was no dramatic change and, as far as I am aware, no explicit call for one that might be compared with Dever's publications in the United States.

A fair conclusion would seem to be that after some delay the factors which I mentioned earlier have seriously weakened the link between biblical studies and archaeology in Britain, even if it has not been broken altogether here and there are more signs of continuing activity in other parts of the world.

Future Prospects

Although it may therefore be more appropriate to speak about a weakened link than about a broken link between the two disciplines, the situation is serious enough to deserve careful evaluation and even some proposals for remedial action. I begin with some comments on the general intellectual situation of the two disciplines at the present time. First, however powerful and in many ways valuable the factors I have mentioned are and have been, they do not by themselves have the ability to serve as total accounts of either the human past, especially in the historical period, or the biblical literature. On the archaeological side the need for a productive but critical interaction between textual studies and the results of excavation has always been recognised in classical and Near Eastern archaeology and no doubt further afield as well. Against the background of the 'New Archaeology' the expression 'historical archaeology' has had to be coined for a way of working which has a long and distinguished pedigree, though I have the impression that it is generally used of more modern periods than those I have men-

---

51 *Century*, pp. 140–3; see also below on his own Schweich Lectures of 2001.

tioned.[52] In any case the key distinguishing feature is the availability of written material. There is excavated written material from ancient Israel, and the study of Hebrew epigraphy and its contribution to biblical studies has much to offer.[53] But its scope and quantity are so far much more limited than one might have hoped, and it is to the Bible that we must continue to look for the majority of our written sources from Palestine itself. Of course they can only serve their purpose if they are subjected to appropriate forms of historical criticism and analysis.

On the biblical side, a purely literary approach to the text cannot provide a fully satisfying account of it any more than a purely theological one can do. To isolate the biblical text from the world in which it emerged is to make it into something which it is not and to forgo many essential clues to its interpretation. Both texts and material culture from the ancient world have much to contribute to a sympathetic reading and a thorough evaluation of the biblical texts. The Schweich Lectures of the past century provide plentiful illustration of this, as do a multitude of other publications, such as the three volumes produced by the Society for Old Testament Study which were noted above (pp. 46–7) and the classic volumes of texts in translation and pictures edited by J. B. Pritchard.[54]

If these considerations justify in principle a continuing interaction between archaeology and biblical studies, it is nevertheless to be expected that the nature and results of such interaction will be significantly, and beneficially, affected by developments within each discipline. And this is, I believe, exactly what we can see happening in the four archaeological series of Schweich Lectures of recent years. Thus, although Othmar Keel's 1998 lectures on 'Symbol Systems of Ancient Palestine in the Light of Scarabs

52 Cf. Trigger, *History*, pp. 535–6 and elsewhere; D. Hicks and M. C. Beaudry, *The Cambridge Companion to Historical Archaeology* (Cambridge, CUP, 2006).

53 See e.g. my essays 'Hebrew Inscriptions', in J. Barton (ed.), *The Biblical World* (London and New York, Routledge, 2002), 1, pp. 270–86; and 'Some Uses of Writing in Ancient Israel in the light of Recently Published Inscriptions', in P. Bienkowski et al. (ed.), *Writing and Ancient Near Eastern Society: Papers in Honour of Alan R. Millard*, Library of Hebrew Bible/Old Testament Studies 426 (London, T. and T. Clark, 2005), pp. 155–74.

54 J. B. Pritchard (ed.), *Ancient Near Eastern Texts Relating to the Old Testament* (Princeton, Princeton University Press, 1950; 3rd edn with supplement, 1969); *The Ancient Near East in Pictures Relating to the Old Testament* (Princeton, Princeton University Press, 1954; 2nd edn with supplement, 1969); also W. W. Hallo and K. L. Younger, *The Context of Scripture*, 3 vols (Leiden, Brill, 1997–2002).

and similar Seal-Amulets' have not (yet) been published, his general approach is well enough known from other publications.[55] The title of the lectures fits well into the language of modern social anthropology and the archaeology which is influenced by it. Indeed it is tempting, even if Keel did not do so himself, to associate his lectures with the 'post-processual' approach to archaeological interpretation represented by authors such as Ian Hodder, which has gone beyond the primarily materialist horizons of early 'New Archaeology' to explore the ideas and beliefs implied by evidence such as that studied by Keel.[56] Again, Roger Moorey's lectures (2001) are a comprehensive study of terracotta figurines from the ancient Near East.[57] The title, 'Idols of the People', is somewhat misleading, as Moorey constantly argues against the view that these figurines are representations of deities, although they have a religious purpose in a broad sense. Correlations with the Bible are notably lacking: it is emphasised that such objects are not referred to in the Bible, they are a case where 'material culture provides evidence absent from the literary tradition' (p. 1) and it informs us about religious practices which were widespread (not only in Israel) but passed over by the 'idealist' and 'elitist' writers of the Old Testament (ibid.). The survey and interpretation of these objects picks up various facets of 'New Archaeology' (the wide scope of the enquiry, though it is not world-wide; the consideration of social as well as religious function; and the use of ethnographic studies [pp. 6–7]), but it is to one of its more recent modifications that Moorey is closest, like Keel. He refers to this as 'cognitive archaeology' (p. 5) and to assemblages of figurines as 'originally constituents of a single system of symbols' (p. 3).[58]

Lawrence Stager's 2004 lectures on his excavations at Ashkelon (which will shortly be ready for publication) presented a more concentrated application of modern methods of interpretation to a single project, combined with older approaches. While maintaining a historical concern with the distinct Canaanite, early Philistine and later Philistine phases of occupation,

---

55 See especially O. Keel, *The Symbolism of the Biblical World* (London, SPCK, 1978), and O. Keel and C. Uehlinger, *Gods, Goddesses and Images of God in Ancient Israel* (Edinburgh, T. and T. Clark, 1998), both of which use pictorial evidence from the ancient Near East itself to clarify ideas and beliefs found in contemporary texts.

56 I. Hodder, *Reading the Past* (Cambridge, CUP, 1986; 3rd edn, 2003).

57 P. R. S. Moorey, *Idols of the People : Miniature Images of Clay in the Ancient Near East* (Oxford, OUP for the British Academy, 2003).

58 Cf. Trigger, *History*, pp. 491–94, who cites as one example S. J. Mithen, *The Prehistory of the Mind: A Search for the Origins of Art, Religion and Science* (London, 1996).

they used scientific analysis of plant remains and bones and geographical systems to map both the family structure of this coastal city and its economic relations with the hinterland and with foreign trading partners. The contrast with Yadin's lectures on Hazor is very evident in these newer features, as well as in the absence of any interest in 'proving the Bible right'.[59] Finally, Dennis Pardee's lectures on the Ugaritic texts in 2007 brought the comparative perspective to bear precisely on literary aspects of those texts and of the Old Testament, thus mirroring a major interest of recent biblical study but placing it firmly within the context of a closely related literary corpus from the ancient Near East.

I should like to amplify a little what I said about Lawrence Stager, because he is one of the major leaders in what one might call a 'New Biblical Archaeology', in a broader sense than simply as the excavator and interpreter of a single ancient site in 'the biblical world'. In a recently published essay in a volume in memory of Yigael Yadin, Stager provides a brief autobiographical account of his own encounter with the 'New Archaeology' in the early 1970s and his efforts to bring the new and the old together, as well as his own assessment of developments outside and inside biblical archaeology.[60] He treads a careful path between 'ahistorical anthropology' and 'humanistic history', but there is no mistaking his openness and enthusiasm for the new: 'In the search for great men and great events amid the rubble of the tells, "ordinary things" that constitute the bulk of the archaeological yield and provide a picture of daily life were neglected. Too often the problem posed could not be solved by the archaeological data recovered.' His own influential essay on 'The Archaeology of the Family in Ancient Israel' and his book (with Philip J. King) on everyday life in biblical Israel more generally illustrate very well what can be achieved with the help of the new methods.[61] This is also evident in the writings of

---

59 For Stager's own conception of the contribution of archaeology to biblical studies see further below. The philosophy of the Ashkelon excavation and its interpretation is very evident in the first volume of the final report: L. E. Stager, J. D. Schloen and D. M. Master, *The Leon Levy Expedition to Ashkelon. Ashkelon I: Introduction and Overview (1985–2006)* (Winona Lake, Eisenbrauns, 2008), esp. ch. 11–13.

60 'Yigael Yadin and Biblical Archaeology', in *In Memory of Yigael Yadin (1917–1984): Lectures Presented at the Symposium of the Twentieth Anniversary of His Death* (Jerusalem, Institute of Archaeology at the Hebrew University and Israel Exploration Society, 2006), pp. 13–27 (quotation from p. 16).

61 *Bulletin of the American Schools of Oriental Research* 260 (1985), 1–35; *Life in Biblical Israel* (Louisville, Westminster John Knot, 2001).

others who have focused more narrowly on the interpretation of the material evidence, such as the contributors to a recent volume edited by Thomas Levy. The work of several younger Israeli scholars deserves special mention, as it is no longer true that Israeli archaeology as a whole lags behind the more recent general developments in the subject.[62]

But history will not go away, and it is ironic that the loudest voice declaring this in recent years in the Near Eastern field has been that of William Dever, whom we have already noted as being one of the leading champions of the 'New Archaeology' and a prominent critic of the old, history-based 'Biblical Archaeology'. Already early in the 1990s Dever was ready, in line with a growing trend in general archaeological thinking, to reopen the dialogue and to speak of a 'rebirth' of Biblical Archaeology.[63] One effect of this was that 'it made history-writing respectable once again' in Dever's eyes.[64] Of course, as Dever himself put it, the question is 'What kind of history?', and in his more recent discussion of the issue one continues to hear his well-worn tirades against the 'diminishing results' of textual studies and the 'bare-bones "political history"' to which they lead.[65] But, while Dever can give his own very illuminating account of social structures and social history,[66] he has in practice shown no reluctance to enter into discussion, and indeed very positive affirmations, about the historicity of particular episodes such as the United Monarchy of David and Solomon and the conquest of Judah by the Assyrian king Sennacherib.[67] There is little doubt that what has drawn him into this—he makes no secret of it—is the rise of the so-called 'revisionist' or 'minimalist' school of biblical historians in Europe, who have denied that there ever was such a 'united monarchy' in Israel. But quite apart from William Dever, there are healthy signs else-

---

62 T. E. Levy (ed.), *The Archaeology of Society in the Holy Land* (New York, Facts on File, 1995); I. Finkelstein, *The Archaeology of the Israelite Settlement* (Jerusalem, Israel Exploration Society, 1988); and more recently, e.g. A. Faust, *Israel's Ethnogenesis: Settlement, Interaction, Expansion and Resistance* (Approaches to Anthropological Archaeology: London, Equinox, 2006).

63 Cf. *Anchor Bible Dictionary* 1 (1992), 354–67, 'Archaeology, Syro-Palestinian and Biblical', esp. pp. 364–6; 'Biblical Archaeology Today: Death and Rebirth', in A. Biran and J. Aviram (ed.), *Biblical Archaeology Today, 1990* (Jerusalem, Israel Exploration Society, 1993), pp. 706–22.

64 Dever, *What Did the Biblical Writers Know?*, p. 66.

65 Ibid., pp. 75, 90.

66 Cf. ibid., pp. 159–244.

67 Ibid., pp. 91–5, 124–38.

where that the contribution of archaeology to the history of ancient Israel is once again being appreciated positively. I will mention just three. A recent symposium sponsored by the British Academy and held on its premises, which dealt with all kinds of sources for the history of Israel in the ninth century B.C., included two leading Israeli archaeologists (A. Mazar and D. Ussishkin) among the speakers, as well as three others who are specialists in Assyriology and West Semitic inscriptions (M. Geller, A. Kuhrt and A. Lemaire).[68] Secondly, in the article already referred to Joachim Schaper has helpfully distinguished the different ways in which archaeological and textual evidence can relate to one another in the treatment of different periods in the history of Israel. So with the emergence of Israel in Palestine archaeology takes the leading role, whereas for the early monarchy the texts do so, and in the post-exilic period (where evidence of both kinds is sparse and complex) the two have equal importance. This is an important step beyond a 'one size fits all' approach, which simply polarises the argument between sceptics and conservatives.[69] Thirdly, in a recent volume two Israeli archaeologists who have been on opposite sides of recent debates about chronology as well as other matters, Israel Finkelstein and Amihai Mazar, present their current thinking about the main periods of the history of Israel, on the basis of their evaluation of both the biblical and the archaeological evidence.[70] Differences certainly remain between them (not least because of their attachment to different schools of thought in mainstream biblical criticism), but significantly both are seeking to occupy the 'middle ground' between ultra-sceptics and over-confident conservatives.

Conclusion

The subject is then in reasonable health and its prospects in general continue to be good. The 'link' between biblical studies and archaeology is still there. But it is stronger in the United States and in Israel than it is here in Britain. My suspicion is that this is even more true in relation to the New Testament

---

68 H. G. M. Willliamson (ed.), *Understanding the History of Ancient Israel* (Oxford, OUP for the British Academy, 2007).

69 *Zeitschrift für die Alttestamentliche Wissenschaft* 118 (2006), 184–5. Schaper's wide-ranging discussion of historical principles and method, drawing on writers such as Max Weber, Marc Bloch and Moses Finlay, is also most valuable (ibid., pp. 183–5, 188–96).

70 Finkelstein and Mazar, *The Quest for the Historical Israel.*

than it is with the Old Testament. What then might be done to strengthen the link in Britain, in ways that safeguard the requirements of both disciplines? First, in those universities where both disciplines are represented more could be done, at both undergraduate and postgraduate levels, to foster collaborative research and teaching. Interdisciplinary activity is more popular nowadays than it once was, and there would be mutual benefit on both sides. Secondly, more could be done to encourage students on biblical courses at all levels (and perhaps their teachers) to participate as 'volunteers' (the irony of this expression will be lost on no one who has done it) in excavations sponsored by American or Israeli institutions, which often include some teaching as well. It is understandable, in the present political situation, that the Council for British Research in the Levant (the successor of the British School of Archaeology in Jerusalem and the British Institute at Amman for Archaeology and History) has not been able to undertake excavations itself in Israel or the Occupied Territories. But it is often forgotten that one of the Council's main areas of work, the kingdom of Jordan, includes not only the ancient territories of the Ammonites, Moabites and Edomites but also regions in the north of the country where ancient Israelites lived, often referred to as Gilead. The excavation of an Iron Age site or sites in that region could make a major contribution to an aspect of biblical history which is very little known, even to biblical scholars.[71] Thirdly, more encouragement should be given to postgraduates in biblical studies to learn languages such as Egyptian, Akkadian and Ugaritic. Fourthly, biblical archaeology is a subject of wide potential interest to the general public, as the editors of Sunday newspapers seem to know very well. Museum displays can and do make a valuable contribution to the wider dissemination of our much increased knowledge of the world of the Bible. But much more can be achieved through public lectures. The monthly meetings of the Palestine Exploration Fund and the Anglo-Israel Archaeological Society have an important part to play in this. But so do the Schweich Lectures, the object

---

71 For a brief review see M. Ottosson, in *Anchor Bible Dictionary*, ed. D. N. Freedman et al. (New York, Doubleday, 1992) 6 vols, vol. 2, pp. 1020–2 (with lit.); more fully id., *Gilead, Tradition and History*, Coniectanea Biblica, Old Testament Series 3 (Lund, Gleerup, 1969); S. Mittmann, *Beiträge zur Siedlungs- und Territorialgeschichte des nördlichen Ostjordanlandes*, Abhandlungen des Deutschen Palästina-Vereins 2 (Wiesbaden, Harrassowitz, 1970); B. MacDonald, *"East of the Jordan": Territories and Sites of the Hebrew Scriptures* (Boston, American Schools of Oriental Research, 2000), pp. 195–208.

of the generous and far-sighted endowment whose centenary has recently been celebrated: indeed the three-lecture format provides the opportunity for a much more comprehensive treatment of a topic than a single lecture can do. It is regrettable that they now take place only every three years, when there is still a long list of subjects on which expert voices ought to be and could be heard, especially if the New Testament as well as the Old is borne in mind. It is to be hoped that the British Academy may, in the context of this centenary, soon find it possible to revert to a regular biennial sequence of lectures, and even one day restore the annual lectures as intended by the original benefactor.

Index of Names